The Wildlife-Friendly Vegetable Gardener

Wildlife-Friendly Vegetable Gardener

How to Grow Food in Harmony with Nature

Tammi Hartung

Author of *Homegrown Herbs*

Illustrations by Holly Ward Bimba

Storey Publishing

The mission of Storey Publishing is to serve our customers by publishing practical information that encourages personal independence in harmony with the environment.

Edited by Carleen Madigan and Elizabeth P. Stell
Art direction and book design by Mary Winkelman Velgos
Text production by Jennifer Jepson Smith

Illustrations by © Holly Ward Bimba
Author's photograph by © Saxon Holt/PhotoBotanic

Indexed by Nancy D. Wood

Storey Publishing
210 MASS MoCA Way
North Adams, MA 01247
www.storey.com

Printed in the United States by Versa Press
10 9 8 7 6 5 4 3 2 1

Library of Congress Cataloging-in-Publication Data

Hartung, Tammi, 1961–
  The wildlife-friendly vegetable gardener : how to grow food in harmony with nature / by Tammi Hartung.
      p. cm.
  Other title: How to grow food in harmony with nature
  Includes index.
  ISBN 978-1-61212-055-3 (pbk. : alk. paper)
  ISBN 978-1-60342-865-1 (ebook)
  1. Vegetable gardening. 2. Gardening to attract wildlife. I. Title. II. Title: How to grow food in harmony with nature.
  SB320.9.H37 2014
  635—dc23
                                    2013030538

*Dedicated to the Earth
and all the lessons she teaches me*

Acknowledgments

I feel deep gratitude for all the wild creatures that live with me in a positive and good way here on our farm. I appreciate that they live on this land or visit it often as part of their daily lives. They offer me great assistance by pollinating the plants, managing pests, and leaving behind their manures to nourish the soil. My gardens would not be so abundant without them.

I offer my heartfelt thanks to Carleen, my editor at Storey. She has been a guiding force to me for some years now and has become an honored friend. All of the Storey staff have been amazing and wonderful, and I thank each and every one of them for their great help and support, with a special thank-you to Liz.

My greatest thanks are for Chris, the amazing love of my life, who has gone out of his way to facilitate the time and space for me to write this book. Thanks also to M'lissa, my lovely daughter, and Lizz, who is like a daughter to me; these two women bring great pleasure and love into my life, and they have both helped me write this book in too many ways to count.

Contents

Preface

My interest in wildlife was nurtured early on, in taking hikes with my father; as we walked along, Dad would point out the animals and trees around us. My maternal grandmother had a special relationship with wild critters, as well. She would talk about them as though they were part of her family, and indeed wild animals always seemed to accept her as part of their world. I remember when a mother raccoon brought her family into the backyard and waited for my grandmother to step out onto the porch and coo over the little ones. After receiving her praise, the mother raccoon herded her children off. My grandmother taught me to be quiet and watch, to respect wild animals, and to honor their role on Earth.

In 1994 I married Chris and moved to the arboretum he managed for the Denver Botanic Gardens. This 700-acre historic farmstead and nature preserve was absolutely teeming with wildlife, large and small. There were coyotes and mountain lions, great horned owls and golden eagles. We had tremendous numbers of deer, including a handsome buck I fondly called Sebastian. I chased that buck out of the 3-acre pumpkin patch on a couple of different occasions. He would stand very still, close to the nature trails, and schoolchildren visiting the arboretum stopped in their tracks, pointing at him when they saw him. I think he enjoyed the attention we all gave him, along with our great respect. For many of those kids he was their first up-close-and-personal experience with a wild animal.

Living at the arboretum, surrounded by wildlife, served as my introduction to wildlife-friendly food gardening. I planted vegetable gardens around our home, which sat in the heart of the historic farmstead. Because our home was located along the pathways open to visitors, Chris's supervisors asked that we not put a fence around my vegetable gardens, which had transformed our front yard. My gardens were also directly in the traffic flow of deer, raccoons, bears, coyotes, and zillions of cottontails. I learned it is not wise to have an open compost pile right outside the kitchen door if there are raccoons in the neighborhood. I discovered that if I planted a parsley border around the garden, the rabbits would eat the parsley and leave the lettuce alone. The deer, too, ate the parsley but not the tomatoes or squash. I gained a lot of firsthand experience in the two years I lived there before we bought our farm and moved to southern Colorado.

We created Desert Canyon Farm, in 1996, to grow organic herbs. Our farm is small, only 5 acres, and sits in a rural neighborhood just minutes from public acreage owned by the Bureau of Land Management (BLM). We are surrounded by other small farms that have horses, goats, cows, and lots of fences. Our farm has only one small fence around a section of the food garden where I grow lettuce and greens. We live with deer, foxes, coyotes, bears, bobcats, and even a bald eagle. There are smaller animals, too — skunks, raccoons, squirrels, and cottontails. The diversity of native pollinators and beneficial insects visiting the farm is staggering.

Our farm is certified as both a wildlife sanctuary and a botanical sanctuary. We offer education to schoolchildren and tours for adults, enabling them to experience a certified-organic working farm in harmony with the natural world. We do not have livestock — only our cats, which we have trained to be wildlife-friendly — so there are no real threats from domestic animals to the wildlife that exists here with us.

The land on our farm was terribly abused as a rental property, but we have slowly turned it into

Coexisting with wildlife in a way that still allows us to earn our livelihood has meant that we need to be very good at observing nature; it has also meant learning a different way of doing things.

and places to build their homes and raise their young. Coexisting with wildlife in a way that still allows us to earn our livelihood by farming crops and growing beautiful productive gardens has meant that we need to be very good at observing nature. Making it all work has meant learning a different way of doing things. I have discovered that some things — like the parsley and the cottontails — work very well, whereas other things have failed miserably. Once, I sprinkled blood-meal as a repellent barrier around a section of my food garden to keep the deer from nibbling there. I was trying to be frugal, so instead of buying a blood-meal product that was formulated as an animal repellent and deodorized, I just bought a bag of regular blood meal. A couple of neighbor dogs smelled the blood meal and destroyed that section of my food garden with their digging. I learned my lesson: to make sure I'm using the most appropriate product for a given situation. In any case, Chris and I have come to believe that gardening with wildlife will be a lifelong learning process, and it is one that we embrace enthusiastically.

I hope you, too, will receive great joy from growing fruits, vegetables, herbs, and flowers in a positive relationship with nature. Having wildlife in my gardens has taught me much about the natural cycles that are occurring around me. I have reaped the gifts of many abundant harvests as the result of all those creatures going about their life work. Words can barely do justice to the richness of my daily experiences in my homeplace, because of the creatures that also make it *their* homeplace. So may it be for you!

With green thoughts,

a paradise that I love to call my homeplace. Chris and I have planted trees by the hundreds, because when we moved here there were only a few. As the trees have grown, so have the varieties of animals and birds. At one point I counted 58 kinds of birds that live or visit here, and each year I see more birds.

One of our goals is to coexist with the wildlife on the farm in a way that meets the needs of the natural world as well as our own. To this end, we constantly strive to create habitats for wild animals that offer protection, food sources, water,

Tammi Hartung

Introduction

Many people these days are passionate about growing their own fruits and vegetables — both to produce food that tastes better and to avoid the potentially harmful chemicals often used in conventional agriculture. Like other food gardeners, I take the responsibility of organic gardening with utmost seriousness, and I indulge deeply in the pleasure of it. I want to grow delicious, nutritious food in a way that minimizes my impact on the earth and leaves behind a healthy garden.

It's no longer enough to assume that tilling the soil, applying fertilizer, and planting seeds will result in a healthy garden. As we learn more about what's going on in the garden, we begin to understand how important it is to honor the community of microorganisms and other soil-dwelling creatures. The health of your vegetable garden is dependent upon the health of these creatures. We also appreciate how critical it is to create habitats that attract beneficial insects, such as lady beetles, and pollinators such as hummingbirds and bumblebees. Our understanding and appreciation of this will inspire us to plant landscapes that foster all manner of creatures from the wild kingdom. The more we know about nature, the more we can benefit from natural cycles. By understanding these cycles, we can learn to manage challenges that arise in our gardens in ways that cause the least amount of harm.

Unfortunately, some gardeners may think that wildlife-friendly gardening means putting up with lower yields, but this doesn't have to be true. Making the organic garden a wildlife-friendly place can actually increase yields, especially when the garden has an abundance of pollinators or beneficial predators. Birds, frogs, and fish help with pest management. Animal manure contributes to healthy soil. All of this will manifest in a bountiful and beautiful garden.

Observing Nature and Creating Habitats

To help you in your journey toward creating a wildlife-friendly garden, this book invites you to expand your relationship with nature. As a first step, it's important to spend time quietly observing wild creatures in the landscape. As you gain greater knowledge about how the natural world is actually influencing the garden (rather than what you *assumed* was happening), you can then utilize that greater knowledge to create an even more beneficial garden environment, both for the wildlife and for yourself. The outcome is likely to be much more appropriate and satisfying as well as more successful.

A healthy garden begins with planning and implementing a landscape that fosters nature. Proactively planning ways to establish wildlife communities within the boundaries of your garden and the surrounding landscape — above and below the surface of the soil — is critical to the whole process. I will share with you my experiences of how to foster the beneficial relationships you will need in the garden.

Caretaking your garden's soil is the place to begin. Every gardener must make an ongoing commitment to nourish it regularly, adding compost and building up levels of organic matter. This diligence will benefit not only plants, but also the huge community of soil-dwelling creatures and microorganisms, such as beneficial fungi, predator spiders, and earthworms. Taking steps to prepare the soil and then maintain it in a way that will not compact or damage its structure is crucial. In this book, I'll present some useful tips to guide you as you prepare your garden.

Once the soil community has been considered and addressed, the next step to creating a wildlife-friendly garden is to plan which perennial plants will create the backbone of the garden and surrounding area. Trees, shrubs, vines, and perennial herbs and vegetables provide a significant advantage for actively inviting pollinators and beneficial predators into the garden habitat. Within the pages of this book, I will introduce you to these helpful creatures and explain how you can welcome them into your landscape.

Creating wildlife habitats such as hedgerows, ponds, and browsing areas can make a tremendous difference in how well your garden and wild communities coexist. These and other strategies for making the garden a welcome place for larger animals are important to include in your garden plan.

In chapter 8 are wildlife-friendly garden designs I put together to entice you, and to offer you a starting point as you plan your own garden. Each design will give insights as to how you can encourage wildlife within your garden and the surrounding landscape, in ways that work with nature while still providing you with abundant harvests. I have partnered each design with a list of plant suggestions, which are not exhaustive by any means. These designs and plant lists are intended only to inspire you. Please adapt, rearrange, add to them — make them your own for your own specific gardening situation.

Knowing When and How Much to Intervene

Embracing wildlife in my garden is mostly very rewarding for me, but at times challenges arise, such as slugs devouring the lettuce patch. The question is how to meet the challenge while causing the least amount of harm. When a problem crops up in the garden landscape, it's easy to overreact. An action that solves the problem in the short run may not be best in the long run. The key is to become competent about when and how much to intervene. I'll give you a repertoire of appropriate responses to consider and try so you can manage problems in ways that return the garden to a place of greater balance. There is a whole toolbox of simple remedies for common pest problems that can solve them pretty easily. When a challenge is greater, there are physical barriers you can utilize to exclude troublesome wildlife from at least a portion of the garden.

The best way to proceed is not always obvious. Sometimes a likely strategy fails miserably. When that happens, try plan B or sometimes even plans C and D. If you can stay calm and collected, you will be better able to determine the most successful course of action, or to invent a brand-new strategy.

Nature is diverse. The beautiful tapestry of life on Earth is woven with threads of various lengths, colors, and textures. Growing your own fruits and vegetables is a perfect example. This year's squash may grow differently next year, because one or more of the pieces that contribute to its growth — the weather, soil nutrients, water, even the seed source — may be different. Each plant, each wild creature, every cycle, represents a thread in the weaving. All add to the richness and resilience of the tapestry, making it beautiful and holding it all together. When you commit to the goal of gardening with nature, you will accomplish a bountiful harvest. But in addition, you receive something even more wonderful: the experiences that nature, and especially wildlife, can bring to your life.

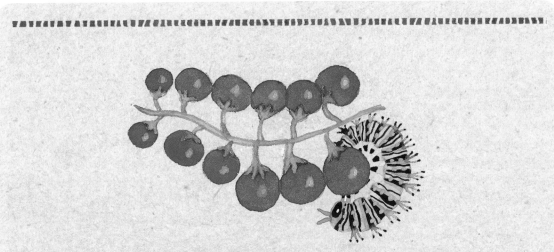

Seeing on a Smaller Scale

A large magnifying glass can help you see what is happening in a very small wildlife community, such as a handful of soil. You will be able to see small creatures that live in the soil and observe their behavior. You might also see tiny seeds that are waiting for the proper conditions to manifest so that they can germinate.

A magnifying glass is an excellent tool for watching insects, especially tiny ones. Once I noticed that the horned tomato caterpillars were covered with tiny white rice-shaped bits all over their backs. I wasn't really sure what was going on, so out came my magnifying glass. I discovered that parasitic wasps (which are tiny) had laid eggs on the caterpillar's body and the eggs had hatched into larvae. The white rice-shaped pieces were the wasp larvae, and they were actually devouring the caterpillar as they grew. I didn't need to handpick the caterpillars off the plants, and, more important, I didn't need to use an organic pesticide. The larvae of the wasps took care of the whole situation efficiently, and as nature intended, keeping my tomato plants safe. The larvae did take a small amount of time to handle the task and so I lost a few tomato leaves to the foraging caterpillars before they died, but the loss was not serious and my tomato plants survived with little harm.

Enough is enough. Thus far and no farther. Think of your children. Of their children. Of the hawks, buzzards, lizards, bear. Save a little room and time for the free play of the human spirit and the wild play of the animal kingdom.
— EDWARD ABBEY

1 Rethinking Our Relationships with Nature

IN THE GARDEN, one natural event may seem to be isolated, but only at first glance. All the plants, animals, soil, water, and weather create circumstances and events in the garden that will affect everything else. Some effects will be obvious; others may seem invisible. Your task is simply to observe and understand the natural cycles enough to interact with them and embrace them, or at the very least to accept them with an attitude of tolerance and patience.

One of the things to understand in wildlife-friendly food gardening is that there will be imperfection and impermanence. The natural world is not tidy or well ordered. It's even downright messy at times! Romantic visions of a perfectly neat, no-leaves-unmunched food garden are unnatural. Strive to work with the natural cycles rather than against them. Embrace imperfection and impermanence, and maybe even a bit of chaos at times, as part of working with natural processes.

Identify Wildlife in the Garden

To grow food gardens in the company of wildlife, you need to identify the communities of animals and insects you see, and learn what they eat and when they appear. It's also important to remember that the mere appearance of wildlife is not necessarily a problem. For example, many homeowners install plantings to attract wildlife they appreciate, such as butterflies and hummingbirds. If you appreciate those, you can learn to admire — or at least develop a more realistic approach to — other wild creatures. And by taking the time to observe their habits, you'll develop a much better working knowledge of these wild creatures.

I used to see birds in my lettuce and kale patch, and I jumped to the conclusion that they were eating my greens. Upon closer observation, I realized they were curve-billed thrashers picking off ants! The ants had been farming aphids on the lettuce, so allowing the birds to remove the ants helped reduce the number of aphids. (In fact, more than 50 percent of a thrasher's diet consists of insects, especially ants.)

Bugs Aren't All Bad

With regard to insects and other bugs, don't assume that any you glimpse in the garden are causing problems. Not all bugs are evil. Determine whether a bug is truly a pest or is instead a good pollinator or a beneficial predator (see chapter 4). Then watch to see what is happening before you do anything. It could be that the beetle you assumed was eating your vegetables is actually pollinating the flowers so that you will have good squash or peppers or cucumbers to harvest later.

If you see caterpillars eating leaves of dill or parsley plants, you might be tempted to pluck them off or go get some pesticide. But take a moment to understand why the caterpillars are there in the first place. Are the caterpillars green with black bands and yellow spots? If so, they are the larvae of beautiful black swallowtail butterflies. The butterflies laid eggs on the dill or parsley plants so that the caterpillars would have food as soon as they hatched. The caterpillar stage is pretty short, lasting a couple of weeks at most. Once a caterpillar is mature, it forms a chrysalis. The caterpillar will stay in the chrysalis stage for several weeks or a few months (depending on the season), during which time it transforms into a butterfly. When it emerges from the chrysalis, the new butterfly won't be eating the dill or parsley. Butterflies feed on the nectar of flowers, in the process pollinating those flowers so that they can mature into fruits such as apples and blueberries, which we harvest for our table. You can't have butterflies without first having caterpillars. Besides, the dill and parsley plants will soon grow plentiful new leaves.

You can see many such cycles happening in the garden landscape throughout the year. As one season yields to the next, the cycles shift and change, each bringing another important piece of the puzzle into view. In spring, snowmelt and rain nourish new plant growth. Plants emerging from winter dormancy protect spiders and insects from predators. Fattening buds erupt into spring blooms that provide pollen, usually around the time when pollinating insects emerge. Migrating birds arrive, badly in need of a rich, nutritious food supply to replenish themselves as they prepare to find mates and raise their young. Newly hatched insects are the perfect food supply.

Birds Can Be Helpers

Throughout the year, birds forage on seeds and insects. They may be feeding on seed heads left on plants in your garden or on seeds from bird feeders you have provided. They might be fattening up on ants in the grass, or gorging when a particular insect population booms in the garden. I've seen birds stuff themselves with pear slugs and grasshoppers in the heat of summer. Birds eat a lot of bugs and can quickly tame a problem situation. Moreover, their droppings enrich the soil. Some of the seeds they disperse will sprout into plants that may improve the landscape. My experience with having a large community of wild birds in the gardens, and all over our farm, is that we rarely need pesticides (organic, of course). The birds typically manage a problem, taking care of matters quickly and efficiently.

I encourage you to find out more about the wildlife that lives in and visits your own garden landscape. You'll soon discover how working with, rather than against, nature can enhance

Living with Skunks

Chris and I have a skunk family that lives on our property, and we enjoy watching them lumbering along at dawn and dusk to get a drink from the pond. After they have their drink, they go about minding their own business, and so do we. We've learned that skunks are not as problematic as people often assume, providing we're careful not to startle or corner them. They're actually quite docile. They sometimes forage at the base of the bird-feeder stations in my gardens, but they don't cause a lot of trouble. This might not be true if you keep chickens, as skunks do sometimes get a taste for chicken eggs and try to raid the hen house. However, a well-built chicken coop should prevent that from being a problem.

your skills as an organic, earth-friendly food gardener. To supplement the information given in this book, I have included some resources and learning tools at the back. Various schools and organizations, county extension services, botanical gardens and arboretums, and community gardening groups offer any number of workshops and seminars. Make use of appropriate resources the next time you're trying to address a pest problem in your garden.

Learn to Be a Good Observer

So how do you begin to shift your thinking about wildlife in your garden? Start by placing your chair in front of a window that overlooks your garden landscape. The next time you drink your morning coffee, afternoon tea, or evening glass of wine, park yourself in the chair and just watch what's going on outside. You'll see birds and other creatures you never noticed before. You'll key in to what that squirrel is really doing in your garden: it's probably burying an acorn, not digging up your green beans. Notice that bumblebee: Which flowers does it fly to and pollinate and which does it seem to ignore? When you simply sit and observe, you begin the process of learning all sorts of things about animals and what they do in your yard and gardens. It's a lifetime process and a tremendous gift to yourself. Encourage your children and grandchildren to participate, too!

Create a Sitting Place

After watching from your window for a while, you'll want to move outdoors. Place a bench or a small table and chair in your garden where you can sit and watch the goings-on. If you sit quietly, wildlife will often get used to your presence and accept it. This is also an excellent way to observe

where problems exist or might come to be. For example, putting up a nest box for solitary bees (i.e., bee species that, unlike honeybees, are not communal) in a tree near a birdbath could result in the bees becoming snacks for the bathing birds. Better to put the bee box in a different part of the garden landscape.

Consider building a bird blind out of bamboo or another material and incorporating small viewing windows. You can also buy a ready-made bird blind if you prefer. By sitting or standing behind the blind, ever so quietly, you can observe what is going on with the birds and other wildlife. This is also a great way to take photographs of birds and other animals in the garden without disturbing them. I've observed young squirrels romping in my pear tree and have seen fawns curled up only a few feet away from me on the other side of our blind.

Time Well Spent

Observing nature as it is happening in the garden and trying to put events together is like fitting the pieces in a giant puzzle. Time is always in short supply, but if you truly hope to interact with nature in a way that benefits all concerned, it's important to go outdoors frequently to observe. Spending even just 5 or 10 minutes a day will teach you invaluable lessons. Leave the computer and the phone inside, and take with you only binoculars or nothing but your own two eyes. When the weather permits, perhaps you can have meals outdoors to continue observing in the garden landscape. Each of these short stints will give you the opportunity to place another piece of the puzzle.

Children especially love spots in the garden where they can hang out to watch the birds or toads or rabbits; the sitting spot can even become their own secret place. Some children love to draw what they see happening around them, so a small table is a perfect addition to a sitting area. Welcoming and encouraging children to participate in quiet observation teaches them understanding, tolerance, patience, and deep respect for wildlife. This also works for adults, particularly those whose lifestyles do not often expose them to wildlife in such a close, personal way.

In my landscape I have a number of sitting areas with chairs and sometimes a small table. As I sit there quietly sipping my cup of tea, I get to watch all the magical happenings around me. I find this experience to be very useful as I design garden spaces. It has also proved to be quite helpful when I'm trying to decide where to situate a birdhouse or a fishpond.

Keep a Nature Journal

One tool I have found to be indispensible is my nature journal. For the past 10 years I have been recording what I see happening in the natural world around me. I write often, though not always daily. The results have amazed me! My nature journal has taught me more about gardening in partnership with wildlife than any other tool I use.

What you write in your nature journal is up to you. I start each entry with the date and the location about which I am writing. Usually the location is my homeplace, but sometimes I write about what I see on a walk at the river or during a car trip or elsewhere in my neighborhood. I like to record what the weather is like on that day and what phase the moon is in. Then I write about what I see happening. I record which plants are blooming or ready to harvest, what is happening in

the bird community, what large animals are hanging around, and what they are doing. I note who has had babies or is about to, or when the young birds are fledging. I jot down which pollinators and beneficial predators are around in the garden landscape, or if there is an outbreak of a pest.

I like to note when it rains or snows, and how much, and during the growing season I make notes about how often I am watering the gardens. Whenever I harvest anything, I mention this in my journal entry, along with any planting or major weeding that is happening. If I install a wildlife home or feature like a birdbath or deer drinking fountain, I mark it in my journal.

You will quickly discover what you like to record in your journal, but keep in mind that it is not just a record of what is going on at any certain time. The journal becomes a tool you can review at will to remind you what took place and when, even if it was months or years before. Chris and I often pull out my old nature journals to help us remember things like what day the apricot trees bloomed the year before or when we noticed the grosbeaks had arrived for the summer several years past.

I suggest that you keep your nature journal free of personal stuff, so that you can make it available to whoever might like to read through it. Mine usually sits in the kitchen sitting area, where visitors who come into that space can read it, and frequently they do! The inside cover page simply states that the journal is personal but not private, and anyone is welcome to read my observations of the natural world. In addition, I have recorded the beginning date on this page and will eventually write in the last entry date, so that any reader will know what period the journal reflects.

I use my nature journal to help me plan and design garden spaces and decide when to plant. I use it to remind me when the flea beetles arrived and started devouring my broccoli, and how

started seeds for the garden. raked out raised beds and turned over compost

Choose a Nature Journal to Suit Your Style

For me, keeping a nature journal starts with selecting a beautiful book with great care, joy, and anticipation at the beginning of each year. I love beautiful covers and watermarked pages, especially those with nature designs. I must have lined pages because I always write crooked. The book must be large enough for me to write several paragraphs under each entry, but not so big and bulky that it's awkward to carry, since I often take my journal into the gardens, on hikes, and even on vacations. Journals with dates printed in them don't work for me; I prefer to enter the date myself. That way I can use half a page or several pages per entry, depending on how much I feel like writing on any given day.

Decide what kind of journal will work best for you. Should it simply be a day planner that has enough space under each date to jot a few notes about what you see happening? If you enjoy drawing, how about a journal with blank pages that allows you to make illustrations about what you are observing? Whatever you choose should feel inviting enough that you look forward to journaling and enjoy reviewing your observations.

I addressed the problem (usually by allowing wild birds to forage the pesky insects). I record whether a particular intervention was successful so that I can repeat or avoid that intervention in the future. You'll find keeping a nature journal an invaluable tool for yourself as well.

Catch Them on Camera

Battery-powered cameras activated by a motion sensor will enable you to see animals that visit your garden when you're not around or those that inhabit areas beyond what you can see from your house. You can also set these cameras to take pictures at specified intervals. You can download the pictures onto your computer to view and archive. Some cameras are capable of taking video footage. Others can work at night using an infrared detector. It's fun to review what's been going on in the landscape at night while you're sound asleep. You're likely to find that most animals follow the same pattern or route within their territories each day or night.

We have three cameras that we place in various places around the farm. If we begin to hear the bobcat outside at night, we mount the wildlife camera on a post in the area where we think it is passing through. Our camera has shown mule-deer bucks sparring with one another as they vie for the attention of does in mating season. The cameras have helped us see where those rutting bucks are damaging our young trees by rubbing their antlers on the bark. Chris can then put a wire cage around specific trees to protect the bark until the trees are mature enough to withstand the rough treatment from the bucks.

A couple of years ago, the cameras showed that a fox family was hunting at night around the bird-feeding stations in our bird garden and then hanging out in our supply barn during part of the day. It didn't appear that the foxes were living in the supply barn, but we did see scat behind some stacks of supplies, so they had obviously been lingering a great deal.

When we saw evidence of rooting around at the base of the bird feeders, we placed one camera on a fence post pointed to that area of the garden. We hung another camera on a beam in the supply barn in the section where we found the scat. It took only one night to get pictures on both cameras of the foxes: a large, handsome male and a smaller, beautiful female. Once we saw the photos, we realized something about the foxes' routine: they were catching mice around the bird feeders.

We still have seen no evidence of damage in the supply barn where they hang out, and they never seem to be inside when we're coming and going from the building, so we've decided not to restrict their entry into the barn. We are careful to make a bit of noise, perhaps a gentle cough, to announce that we are coming inside whenever we enter the barn from the open walk-through doorway on the west end, especially if we are entering early in the morning or around dusk. If the foxes were in the barn, they would be able to easily exit under the sliding double doors at the opposite end. They still come and go at night from the bird feeders to the barn. Every so often we set up the cameras again, which not only enables us to check on them but also gives us great fox pictures to use on our blog or show to friends and students.

As long as we can coexist with the foxes peacefully, there will be no need to interfere with their routine, and we can take advantage of their supreme hunting skills to manage any rodent activity in our gardens and in the supply barn. If the situation should ever develop into a problem, we will just block their access into the barn. Simply disrupting their routine and making it inconvenient for them to feed or hide can discourage many wild animals from hanging around.

That the sky is brighter than the earth means little unless the earth itself is appreciated and enjoyed.
— HELEN KELLER

2 Encouraging Friends in the Underground

WHEN IT COMES TO YOUR GARDEN'S HEALTH and well-being, caring for the soil is the most important thing you can do. Supporting the layers of soil where plant roots grow is a crucial part of this caretaking, so understanding a little about what's happening underground will help you build good, healthy soil. In addition, you'll want to nurture and protect the community of wild creatures and microorganisms that live underground. They play a critical role in building the soil, and many of them also help to protect the plants in some fashion, be it from pests or from diseases. To this end, consider and make good choices about how you prepare the soil for planting, and then how you will care for it in the future. You'll also need to plan how best to provide and maintain moisture in the soil. The efforts you put into caring for your soil, and the community of creatures that make it their abode, will be well worth the extra time and energy required. In the long run, your hard work will make your garden much more sustainable.

Who's Down There?

Soil is formed in many layers, but from a gardener's perspective, the first four layers are the most important to creating a healthy garden. The top layer is where organic material like leaves, manure, and rotting fruit begins to decay; you can look at this layer and easily tell what the organic material is. In the second layer, the process of decomposition is further along and bits of organic material are more difficult to identify. By the time organic material has made it to the third layer, it's fully decomposed and can no longer be identified by the naked eye. These three layers of soil are where organic materials are broken down by soil-dwelling creatures and microorganisms. The result of this process supplies nutrients to the plants that grow there, contributing to a bountiful harvest. The fourth layer is where water percolates through, carrying organic particles

from the other layers. This layer of soil is where most biological activity occurs and where the highest amounts of organic matter are present. This is the layer where plant roots grow best. Beneath the fourth layer are several more, and then a layer of bedrock. These layers do not contribute as much to growing plants, so they're not of too great an interest to the gardener.

The community of soil-dwelling creatures (many of which aren't visible to the naked eye) is a rich and complex network of beings. Earthworms, which aerate the soil and break down waste materials into nutritious organic matter, are part of this community. Soil also contains healthy bacteria that help to fix nitrogen, along with beneficial nematodes that feed on pest-insect larvae. Beneficial varieties of fungus live in the soil on the roots of plants. A few types have the job of trapping damaging root nematodes, thus

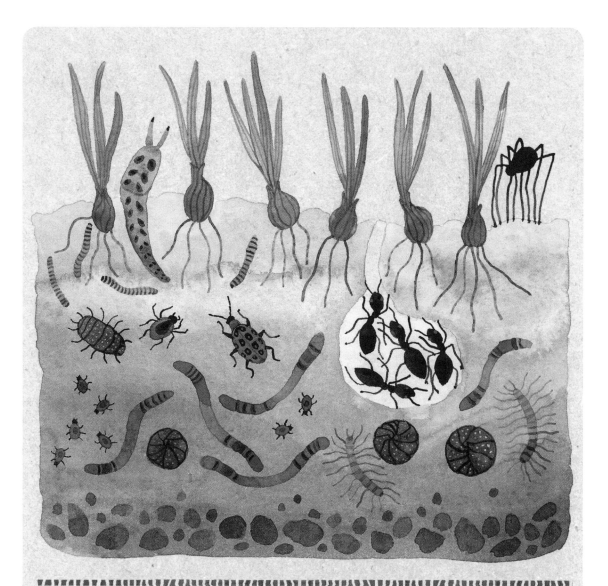

Hire an Earthworm!

Earthworms are fascinating — ask any kid! They are champion soil cultivators. They help break down organic matter in the soil and turn it into rich, nutritious humus that supplies nutrients to plants and soil organisms. In that process, the worms aerate the soil, keeping it loose around the roots of the plants. There can be as many as 50 earthworms in a square foot of healthy soil. Just imagine all the good cultivating work that many earthworms can do! If you own a tiller, remember that using it often will discourage earthworms.

Earthworms provide food for birds. We always think of robins when we talk about the early bird that gets the worm, but many different bird species hunt earthworms as a part of their diet. Earthworms are never a bad thing to have in your soil, whether they are living in your garden or in your lawn.

protecting a plant's roots. Creatures like beetles, spiders, and mites have the very important task of shredding up bits of organic material so that it can be decomposed more efficiently.

Ants, which may seem annoying to humans, are residents of the soil community, and their tunnels help loosen and aerate soil so it doesn't compact. Loose soil helps plant roots establish themselves securely. Slugs are nocturnal members of the soil community, living near the soil's surface, which they frequent at night while eating leaves. The slime trail they leave behind as they travel helps bind soil particles together. There are zillions of these types of relationships going on under the surface of the soil, where we can't see them, but we should be aware that they exist and are doing good work toward a healthy garden. Just like the aboveground wildlife community, the more diversity we encourage, the better!

Build a Healthy Soil Community

How you choose to prepare the garden for planting will have an impact on the soil community, so it's worth putting some careful thought into how you'll proceed. If you have very compacted soil where you plan to put your garden, you'll definitely need to use a more aggressive method to prepare it, such as double digging or rototilling. If you can accomplish your garden preparation using a no-dig method, however, you won't disrupt the structure of the soil community, which will allow your plants to benefit more immediately from all the positive attributes soil-dwelling creatures have to offer.

Once the initial soil preparation has been completed, it's equally important to keep the soil in good condition. Preventing soil from becoming compacted is crucial to how well and how quickly your plants will establish themselves and grow.

Ensuring that your garden soil maintains a good level of organic matter will not only support the plants living in that soil, but will also foster the creatures and microorganisms that live in the soil as well. To that end, providing adequate moisture is something every gardener must have a plan for. Finally, mulching helps keep precious water in the soil, and smothers weeds at the same time.

Work the Soil Gently

Keep in mind that aggressive soil disturbance will cause damage or destruction to the soil community that may take a very long time, sometimes many years, to repair itself. Because of this, it's wise to carefully consider how you're affecting the soil when you prepare your garden beds.

Some gardeners feel that double-digging the soil when the garden is first prepared is the best way. This process — which involves digging a trench, placing the soil off to the side, then digging a second trench and filling the first trench with the topsoil from the second trench — may be helpful for dealing with compacted soil, but it also ends up inverting the layers of soil structure and puts organisms used to dwelling in the topsoil layer down in the subsoil.

Other gardeners prefer to use a rototiller to create new planting areas. A rototiller (i.e., an engine-powered tiller with rotary blades, or tines) is handy for preparing soil that has never been worked or has not been worked for a very long time. It saves time, not to mention wear and tear on your body. Rototiller tines typically do not work the soil as deeply as double-digging does, but rototilling does an acceptable job of breaking up soil so that it's easy to work. You can also spread a layer of compost over the top of the soil about 1 inch deep and mix the compost into the soil as you till.

One word of caution, though: Frequent rototilling can damage soil structure that may have taken years to develop and that is essential for good drainage. Once I have done the initial preparation for a new garden space, I rarely ever till again. I do not want to disturb the healthy soil community of beneficial microorganisms and creatures, such as earthworms.

Using the No-Dig Method to Preserve Soil Structure

Another method of soil preparation — one less aggressive than both double-digging and rototilling — has gained popularity in recent years: the no-dig method. For this technique, the soil is not dug deeply or turned over, and no tilling is done. Indeed, the only disturbance that happens to the soil comes from planting and weeding. Those who practice the no-dig method believe that an established, well-ordered soil community is functioning at a high level of good health and will support all the creatures and plants that live in that soil, both above and below the surface. After observing the health of my garden since I began using this approach several years ago, I've decided it makes the most sense for me.

I do disturb the soil as I am planting or weeding, but not aggressively, and no more often than is really needed to keep the garden in tidy order. I top-dress my soil with composted organic matter that earthworms, ants, and other organisms will mix into the soil for me. Some of the compost will soak into the soil with snowmelt, rain, or watering.

Avoid Compacting the Soil

In an ideal world, you should avoid walking on the soil where your plants are growing. Practically speaking, however, some gardening or harvesting tasks will require you to step in the bed where the plants are growing, so your garden should be designed to minimize soil compaction.

There are many reasons to avoid compaction. With dense soil, plants have difficulty establishing a strong root structure that can range far and wide to extract nutrients. The root structure also supports the portion of a plant growing aboveground. Water cannot easily soak into compacted soil, leaving plants under-hydrated and starved of waterborne nutrients. In addition, the soil community of microorganisms and other beneficial creatures will struggle if the soil they live and work in is hard-packed.

Provide Organic Matter

Organic matter is essential for maintaining soil health and integrity. It provides nutrition for the many kinds of wildlife that live in the soil, which, in turn, provide nutrition for the plants (when they excrete). Organic matter also keeps soil loosened up so that plants can form deep, strong root structures to support themselves. Keeping the soil stocked with organic matter will also help it soak up and retain moisture, like a sponge.

Organic matter can be compost, chopped leaves, and aged animal manure. You can till leafy green cover crops such as oats and winter rye into the soil as another excellent way to build up good levels of organic matter. Compost made in your own pile or barrel is a fantastic way to bring organic matter into the garden soil.

You can tell if soil is on the right track of having enough organic matter by its consistency. Take a handful of slightly moist earth and squeeze it into a fist. When you open your hand, the soil should crumble between your fingers rather than forming a tight ball. If you have sandy soil, this test may not work well, but you

straw and old hay

manure

compost

leaves and grass

Convert Lawn into Garden without Digging

Determine the area you would like to convert from grass into a vegetable garden, then mark the perimeter with flags or stakes. Mow the grass short in this area to facilitate your next layering steps.

First, on top of the grass lay down several layers of newspaper or overlapping pieces of corrugated cardboard, 3 to 4 inches deep if possible. Wet each layer as you go (using a sprinkler or hose) to hold it in place. Next, add a layer of garden soil 3 inches deep. Now cover the entire area with a thick layer of mulch, at least 6 inches deep (8 inches is even better). For mulch, you can use any kind of plant material that will eventually rot: for example, old hay or straw, grass clippings, shredded wood chips, or sawdust.

Your final step is to water the new garden area and let it sit for a solid week, or longer. This will enable the newspaper or cardboard layer to begin to compost. Then your new garden will be ready to plant.

When you're ready to garden, simply pull back the top layer of mulch down to the soil layer and plant your seeds or transplants as you would normally do, but try not to disturb the soil any more than is necessary to accomplish the task. For transplants, replace the mulch around them and you're good to go. If you've sown seeds, don't cover them with the mulch. Instead, move the displaced mulch close to the section or row where the seeds have been sown, leaving the soil over the seeds exposed.

can still inspect the soil in your hand to see if it contains bits and pieces of composted material mixed with the sand.

You should strive for 4 to 5 percent organic matter. If you want to know the exact amount of organic matter present in your soil, pick up a soil sampling kit from your county extension office, follow its instructions on how to take a soil sample, and then take or send the sample to the extension office to have it tested. Be sure to write on the soil sample that you want it tested for the amount of organic matter present.

Maintaining abundant levels of organic matter in the soil is an ongoing process; it will never be a completed task. New areas in the garden may not have very much organic matter in the soil until you start to add it each year. Mix it into the soil during the initial garden-soil preparation, and then supplement with maintenance applications from that point onward. Once the garden is prepared and established, add your compost as a topdressing annually at the beginning of the growing season. It will soak in and nourish the soil as the garden is watered. In this way you will be building healthy soil and replenishing the organic matter as it gets used up by the tiny organisms that convert it to plant nutrients.

If your soil is sandy, if you garden in a hot climate, or if your soil seems to be low in organic matter, spread a second topdressing of compost at the end of the growing season. This extra application will break down over winter, when not much active growing is taking place. Even in regions where the climate allows for year-round gardening, the garden's natural cycle slows down a bit in winter. As the garden soil approaches that ideal mark of 4 to 5 percent organic matter, you'll see the evidence of it in how well your garden is growing and in the good yields you get from your food and herb plants.

A plant that wilts a bit a few times can usually recover well enough, but repeated serious wilting may kill a plant or render it less able to ward off pests and diseases.

Water Well

Planning for adequate water is as important as preparing the soil. Fruits, vegetables, and herbs require adequate water to produce big juicy fruits and seeds with generous harvest yields, and, of course, it is much easier to harvest root crops if the soil is moist rather than very dry. Soil-dwelling creatures such as beneficial nematodes and tiny predator spiders, which lay their egg sacs around the structures of plant roots, cannot survive in soil that has become too dry. Fungal structures that protect plant roots from diseases also require moisture in the soil to live. Some geographic regions receive adequate natural rainfall to support this kind of plant and soil life, but many do not. If there is not enough natural rainfall, you'll need to supplement to ensure that that your fruits, vegetables, herbs, and edible flowers are provided with enough moisture to thrive but are not watered unnecessarily, wasting precious resources. Equally important is to establish how often and for how long to water. Windy sites dry out faster than sheltered gardens. Sandy soils dry out quickly, while those with lots of clay or organic matter won't need watering as often.

Your goal is to keep the plants' root zone evenly moist, neither excessively wet nor bone dry. A good weekly soaking encourages food plants to develop deep, drought-resistant root systems. (Perennial herbs such as thyme and oregano need less; raspberries need more when fruiting.) To take the guesswork out of determining when to water, or until you get a feel for how much your plants are using and how long it takes for them to need water again, a moisture meter is a useful tool. Moisture meters cost $20 or so, and are worth every penny. After using a moisture meter for a while, you will soon learn to gauge when the garden needs water just by hand-testing the soil or observing the plants, noticing whether they are perky or a bit limp or grayish-green.

Frequent, shallow watering results in plants with shallow root systems. Shallow roots give plants less resilience if you face water restrictions or a drought, or if the watering schedule gets disrupted for some reason, such as a vacation. Plants with shallow roots can't draw up needed moisture and nutrients from deep in the soil. If the top few inches of soil dry out, these plants will wilt and struggle to maintain themselves. This can affect the formation of both fruits and vegetables. A plant that wilts a bit a few times can usually recover well enough, but repeated serious wilting may kill a plant or render it less able to ward off pests and diseases.

Overwatering isn't healthy either, as soggy soils can smother roots and encourage disease. Water deeply but not too frequently to encourage

Grow Your Own Organic Matter

For large gardens, it's a challenge to produce enough compost to add to the beds each year. An easy alternative is to plant cover crops, that is, crops grown solely for the purpose of turning them under and adding organic matter to the soil. This process is also called green manuring. If your garden is large enough, you can fill a spare a bed with a cover crop. In smaller gardens, you can plant a cover crop after an early crop such as peas is finished. Each year, I try to leave one area in the garden planted in a cover crop like winter rye during the off-season or oats during the active gardening season. Both of these cover crops will grow fast and can be tilled or dug into the soil while they are young and juicy. Tilled in at this tender stage in their growth, they will quickly decompose, feeding the soil-dwelling community of earthworms and microorganisms.

Winter rye stays green all winter, even with freezing temperatures and deep snow. It has the extra advantage of providing a food supply to the deer in winter, when grazing options are greatly limited, which may reduce browsing damage to landscape plants. The manure the deer leave behind as they are grazing provides additional nutrition to the soil when the winter rye is tilled in.

Oats are great for spring and summer sowing. They will germinate early in spring as soil temperatures are just beginning to warm a bit, and they grow fast. If your garden space is new, consider planting an early-spring crop and tilling it into the soil when the oats are 6 to 8 inches tall. They will break down quickly once tilled in. By the time you are ready to plant your annual heat-loving vegetables like squash or peppers, in late spring, you will have boosted the levels of soil organic matter considerably. In established gardens you can plant areas in oats and hand-dig them into the soil.

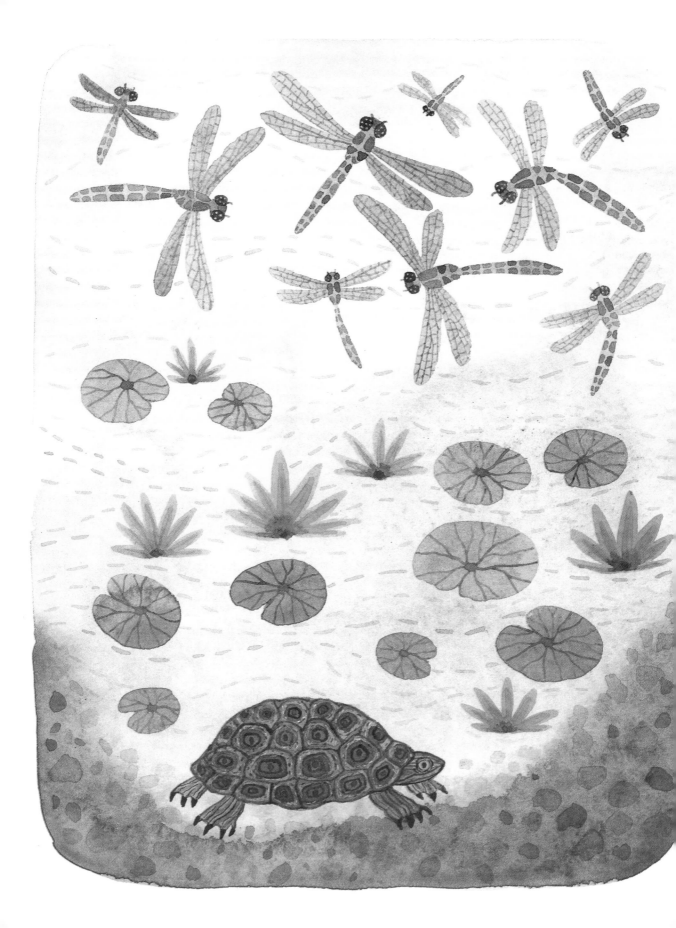

deep root systems to support plants even when heavily laden with fruit and seed, and to keep them healthy enough to withstand attacks by pests and diseases.

Be wise about when and how you water your garden landscape. Water ideally in the morning before the heat of the sun is too intense. That way you lose less water to evaporation and allow plenty of time for the foliage to dry off before nightfall. Wet foliage during cool night hours is a recipe for fungal problems in the garden, especially with susceptible vegetables like tomatoes and lettuce. If the wind is blowing vigorously, choose another time to do your watering. There is nothing helpful about wind blowing the water to areas you don't intend for it to go. Choosing a sprinkler design that does not put out a really high or sweeping spray will also mean less loss to evaporation. Remember to check your rain gauge or moisture meter. If it shows a good amount of moisture, then skip a watering cycle or two. It is not sensible to water if the rain has already accomplished that task for you, and it is just extra work for you.

Another tip: If your yard has a pond that's closer to the garden than a house spigot is, you can pump irrigation water from the pond. Just be sure to maintain the water level in the pond so that fish and wildlife are not at risk of running out of water. The nice thing about running pond water through your drip system is that the water will contain extra nutrients from the fish excretions.

Save That Water!

The high mountain desert of Colorado is a native-plant community of piñon pine and juniper. Rainfall measures about 12 to 15 inches in a normal year. Water conservation is always in the forefront of the mind of everyone who lives here. Many areas face periodic water shortages, even water restrictions. Truly, though, with all the burdens the global environment must contend with, everyone should conserve natural resources regardless of the local climate. Water conservation is only one piece, but an important one, of our responsibility to the planet.

Water conservation means not being stingy with water resources but rather being wise and respectful. Give your plants the water they require, but do not lavish excess water on them. Infrequent deep watering produces healthier, more adaptable plants and uses less water overall than frequent shallow watering. Use the best, most water-conserving delivery method possible. Most of the time the best method is drip irrigation or soaker hoses. Whatever approach you use to water your garden, keep your equipment in good working order. Install manual shutoffs on every one of your hoses so that you can turn the water off as you move hoses to different parts of the garden or between watering containers. You never want the water to be flowing freely where it is not needed.

Keep your soil well stocked with 4 to 5 percent good organic matter, which acts like a sponge to hold moisture in the soil. Use mulch, too, to help hold moisture in the soil. When appropriate, plant perennial food plants such as fruit trees or berry bushes strategically where they will offer shade during the hot afternoon to more vulnerable plants like salad greens. In so doing, it will not be necessary to water those more vulnerable plants as often.

Mulch to Retain Moisture

I am an avid champion of using mulch in food or herb gardens, perennial flower gardens, rock gardens, you name it. Mulching facilitates moisture conservation in the soil, which in turn will help to support the creatures and micro-organisms that live in it. Many beneficial predator insects and ground-nesting pollinators also utilize mulched garden spaces to build their homes. The only time mulch isn't beneficial is when soils tend to be too moist or slugs are too abundant, although a shallow layer of gravel mulch can still be useful in either situation.

Mulch helps hold moisture in the soil around the plants, and this is especially critical in arid climates, like ours in Colorado. No matter where you live, mulch will help decrease the amount of weeding you must do, because fewer weeds will be able to sprout through it. Mulching helps prevent erosion from wind and heavy rains, too. In addition, it provides an attractive cover for pathways in the garden, reducing your mowing while reducing soil compaction. Pathways provide essential access for routine maintenance, but heavy foot traffic and wheeling carts to and fro tend to compact the soil underneath.

What type of mulch you choose for your garden will depend on your preference, your budget, or the availability of mulching materials. Choices include wood chips, nut shells, gravel, and straw or grass clippings.

I tend to use wood chips in most of my gardens, but in the raised beds for vegetables, herbs, and berries, I use barley straw. It's antimicrobial, so it won't foster mold and bacteria growing in or on the soil. I use it around garlic plants, on the strawberry beds, under the squash and cucumber vines, and at the base of tomato and pepper plants.

Where pests have been a problem in the food garden, it is crucial to remove mulch at the end of the growing season. Getting rid of straw mulch in late fall or winter removes some wintering-over insect eggs, such as those of grasshoppers, and exposes others in the soil to freezing temperatures and hungry birds.

Recycle that straw by arranging it around the base of trees and shrubs or under hedgerows well away from the vegetable patch. There it will gradually break down into organic matter and nourish the soil. Old straw mulch also makes a great addition to the compost pile.

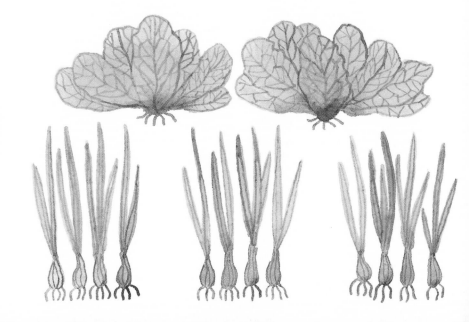

> *What is the purpose of the giant sequoia tree? The purpose of the giant sequoia tree is to provide shade for the tiny titmouse.*
> — Edward Abbey

3 Garden Elements That Welcome Wildlife

A GREAT MANY TREES, shrubs, vines, hedgerows, vegetables, and herbs can serve the garden landscape as backbone plants, establishing a multistory environment that creates microclimates and habitats. They set the stage by welcoming birds, beneficial insects, earthworms, garter snakes, and toads to make their homes and raise their young in and near the food garden.

Trees and shrubs flower before yielding their delicious harvest of nuts, fruits, and berries; the flowers provide fodder for many types of pollinators, including mason bees, honeybees, butterflies, and moths. Berry bushes and asparagus can provide wind protection for more tender plants such as tomatoes and peppers, or midsummer shade for lettuces. The list of perennial food plants is quite long, so you have great variety of choice in what to include in your garden. Keep in mind that you must choose your perennial plants — and their place in the garden — with care. Although you can relocate a rhubarb plant or asparagus patch, it's a lot more work than planting tomatoes in a different spot.

Create a Perennial "Backbone"

Establishing the backbone of your garden requires a bit of careful thought. Select varieties of plants that match your growing conditions; seek out local advice for what grows well in your particular area. County extension services and local nurseries can provide invaluable help for which varieties of fruit or nut trees and bushes will do best with your conditions. You will need to consider hardiness to make sure trees, shrubs, and perennial crops will survive your cold seasons. For example, as much as I would love to have a pecan tree, I know it is too cold and dry here in Colorado for such a tree to thrive. Choose plants that tolerate the typical levels of moisture your region receives from rain or snow. It is important to do a bit of research to make sure you're not selecting varieties that have pest or disease problems that are common in your area.

In Colorado, for example, it's important to choose varieties of apples, plums, pears, and cherries that are resistant to fire blight. Do your research before you purchase any plants so they stand a good chance of thriving where you live.

The perennial food plants that form the permanent backbone of my garden provide me with an ongoing supply of food to fill my pantry each year and, at the same time, have become a crucial part of my total landscape. They add beauty and a sense of peacefulness. They create the flow pattern that inspires where I plant my annual vegetable plants each gardening season. Every year is slightly different from the year before, as I practice crop rotation in the vegetable garden, but those always-present fruit trees, berry bushes, and horseradish provide a sense of consistency. Most important, the same permanent garden community members that provide food to fill my pantry

also create a habitat for the wildlife that shares this land. The animals are a critical part of the natural cycles here. Each contributes an important piece to the process of a thriving, healthy garden and to the larger picture of good earth stewardship.

Trees for Food and Habitat

If your yard is large enough, selecting trees is a great place to begin. While nut trees can take up a huge amount of space, hazelnut and semi-dwarf fruit trees fit in most suburban yards. If all you have is a sunny patio or porch, you may still be able to grow a dwarf fruit tree in a container. In southern Colorado, black walnuts and piñon pines are two possibilities. In other parts of North America the choices might include English walnuts, pecans, almonds, and filberts (hazelnuts).

The list of fruit-tree possibilities is very long, depending on where you live. In Colorado options include apples, peaches, pears, nectarines, apricots, cherries, plums, and the humble yet delicious mulberry. Friends in southern Arizona have lemons, limes, grapefruits, and oranges growing in their gardens. Another friend, in Hawaii, grows papayas, mangoes, avocados, and bananas. (The banana plant is not officially a tree, and is not even considered a true perennial, but most people think of it as a tree.)

Consider carefully the best location for any trees before you purchase or plant them. Make sure you plant them far enough apart to allow for their mature size. Also remember that trees will cast shade. In climates with hot summers, this may be an advantage. Many salad greens grow better with a bit of shade. Even green beans benefit from some afternoon shade where summers are very hot; plant them on the east side of trees or shrubs so they'll get good morning sun.

Fruiting Shrubbery

Once you've made your tree choices, the next step is to consider which bushes to include in and around your food garden. Berry bushes produce a lot of fruit in relatively little space, plus they are easier to harvest from than fruit trees are. I can't imagine a food garden without a generous raspberry patch. Red and black currants are also permanent residents in my garden. Blueberries are some of the easiest fruits to grow, if you can give them the acid soils they require. Other fruiting bushes include elderberry, blackberry, boysen-berry, and gooseberry. Roses are an ornamental addition for their edible hips and flowers; some types produce larger hips than others. Gardeners in tropical and subtropical climates can grow figs if they have enough space in their garden. A row of berry bushes can provide a bit of a windbreak for a vegetable garden, but be careful to locate it far enough away to avoid shading vegetables.

Vines Are Fine

It is quite nice to incorporate perennial vines such as grapes, passionflower, and hops as part of your garden's perennial backbone. Kiwi vines are an option for some climates. Vines are especially appropriate for screening to create privacy for the garden's humans or to cover an unattractive wire fence. A vine-covered arbor or pergola adds a decorative element to a food-producing landscape; in hot climates it can also be designed to provide much-needed shading for plants that are a little less tolerant of hot sun.

Hedgerows Welcome Wildlife

Hedgerows are informal plantings, typically of shrubs, trees, and vines, that supply food and habitat for many kinds of wildlife. They are permanent plantings that will foster beneficial

elderberries

gooseberries

blueberries

raspberries

black currants

boysenberries

rose hips

insects, many types of pollinators, and wild birds. They may also provide homes to larger animals. Such plantings are excellent partners for traditional food gardens, whether planted along the perimeter or nearby. If strategically located, hedgerows can double as windbreaks or even as dust screens in arid regions, offering extra protection to tender vegetables such as greens, tomatoes, and beans. Another gift they offer is simple privacy from the outlying world.

Hedgerows can easily contain berry bushes, rosebushes, nut trees, or other plants that provide tasty treats for humans. Nontraditional fruits such as mulberries, serviceberries (also called Juneberries or saskatoons), and wild plums may fit in best as part of a wildlife hedgerow. Hazelnuts, piñon pines, and hawthorn trees make wonderful additions. For more on hedgerows, see chapter 5.

We planted a hedgerow along the north side of our home, very near the primary food garden and running parallel to a row of wine grapes. Our hedgerow includes Angel Wing roses, which have tiny hips that finches, pine siskins, and other small birds like to feast on in winter. I've also seen some pinyon jays interested in those rose hips during the cold months. There is a maple tree and a seed-grown apple tree. Seed-grown apples are always unpredictable, as one is never sure if their fruit will be large and delicious, small and sour, or something in between. Still, I like to grow apples from seed. Even if this seedling never produces good eating apples, it will still be an excellent addition to our north hedgerow because whatever kind of fruit it does produce will be a useful source of food for wildlife.

Our hedgerow also contains a Manchurian apricot tree, which yields smaller fruit than a typical fresh-eating variety of apricot. The apricots are somewhat tart but still very tasty, and we enjoy eating them fresh. We also dehydrate a bunch of these little apricots, sprinkled with cinnamon and vanilla-infused sugar, to be used as hiking snacks. Chris and I are not big jam eaters, but we have friends who love to make apricot jelly and preserves from Manchurian apricots. These cute and tangy little apricots also make wonderful wildlife food, so much so that I am planting more of these trees in the windbreaks on the perimeter of the farm.

My hedgerows are great gathering places for wild critters. They seek out these plantings because they know there's a source of food there. Wild birds build nests in hedgerows, and squirrels also make their homes there. Animals also use the hedgerows for protection from weather and predators, like the mother deer that leave their fawns hidden away for several hours in the heat of the day. I have placed water sources near some of the hedgerows to make them a one-stop food-and-drink station.

Bad Neighbors

Two types of nuts — black walnuts and butternuts — must be situated with care on any but the largest properties. While both of these large trees produce delicious nuts, their roots give off a substance called juglone that's toxic to some other plants. The roots of these trees extend beyond their branches, so even vegetables growing outside the shade of these trees may not grow well. Tomatoes, potatoes, and cabbages are especially sensitive to juglone.

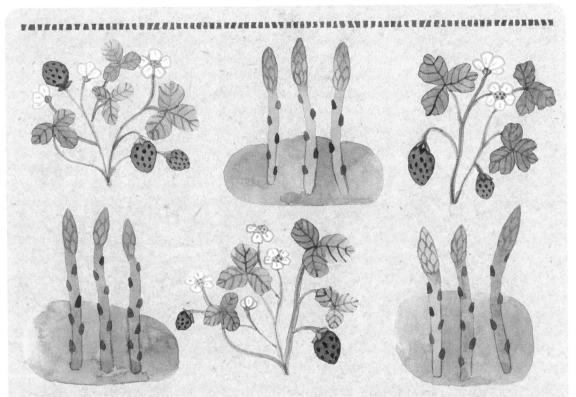

Asparagus and Strawberries: Cozy Companions

A creative and attractive way to grow asparagus and strawberries is to interplant the two in a single raised bed. A 4-foot by 8-foot bed is wide enough for a row of asparagus down the center. Space the plants 12 inches apart. On either side of the asparagus, plant a row of strawberries spaced 8 inches apart.

Over time, as this bed matures, the strawberries will produce runners that will establish themselves and fill in the spaces. Mulching with straw will help hold in moisture, keep down weeds, and keep the strawberry fruits from resting on the soil of the raised bed, which prevents pill bugs (roly-polies) from eating the berries. The straw mulch will also help protect the asparagus and strawberry roots in winter.

The asparagus will send up tender shoots early in spring that can be harvested and sautéed with a bit of garlic and butter for a simple, delicious meal. As the asparagus harvest season starts to wane, the strawberries will have begun to fruit. Each day will bring delicious berries for breakfast with yogurt, walnuts, and a bit of cinnamon.

I prefer to grow everbearing strawberries, my favorite variety being Tristar, but there are a number of good strawberry choices. Everbearing strawberries provide me with an ongoing harvest throughout the late spring and summer and well into autumn. June-bearers will give a large harvest all at once, making them the variety of choice for cooks who want to prepare a plentiful supply of jelly or jam, but these strawberries do not continue to yield fruit the rest of the summer. My neighbor Carol is a fan of June-bearing strawberries because she likes to make a big annual batch of strawberry jam, which she uses as holiday gifts at the end of the year.

rosemary   mint   fennel

Perennial Vegetables and Fruits

Other important pieces of the backbone of the food garden are the smaller but equally critical perennial vegetables and fruits. These provide a predictable food harvest for the pantry, but do not need to be planted each gardening season, the way annuals like beets and eggplants do. In addition, they're important anchors for many beneficial insects and pollinators, especially the ground- and wood-nesting pollinators. Bumblebees use strawberry blossoms as an early source of nectar when temperatures are still too cold for tomatoes or peppers to be flowering. Asparagus, artichokes, sorrel, and fiddlehead ferns are delicious perennial vegetables, so you will enjoy them year after year. Strawberries, rhubarb, and blueberries are tasty additions to the garden space, as they contribute to your dessert menu.

Perennial Herbs

Planting herbs in a food garden is a natural thing to do. It's an efficient use of space to have herbs, fruits, and vegetables growing in among one another. Herbs offer flavoring for the kitchen, tasty teas, and remedies for the medicine cupboard, with the added advantage that they attract many kinds of pollinators and beneficial insects. For example, mint attracts lady bugs, which hunt aphids on your broccoli; at the same time, the mint will repel flea beetles from your kale. Planting a lot of different herbs, such as sage, mint, and fennel, will attract many insect helpers to your garden. The herbs also have lots of volatile oils, which give them great taste and fragrance, but they also repel some kinds of larger wildlife, such as deer and elk, which cannot abide the strong smell. These animals will avoid areas of the garden where herbs like lavender and rosemary are growing. Both perennial and annual herbs are wonderful companion plants to fruits and vegetables for these reasons.

Two herbs are well worth growing in your garden landscape for the benefit they provide to your compost pile: common nettles (*Urtica diocia*) and comfrey. Nettle, which is in fact both a vegetable and an herb, is quite important as a backbone member of the garden. I use nettles in

Herbs That Attract and Repel

- Catnip will attract lady bugs, which are great predators of aphids and whiteflies.
- Chamomile attracts parasitic wasps, which help control worms and caterpillars.
- Comfrey creates wonderful habitat for beneficial spiders.
- Dill and fennel both attract predator wasps.
- Horseradish repels potato bugs, and is excellent habitat for beneficial spiders.
- Garlic repels aphids, tree borers, snails, flea beetles, and squash bugs.
- Mints attract lacewings and lady bugs, which are great general predators. They also repel flea beetles, cabbage flies, and mosquitoes.
- Oregano repels aphids and attracts lady bugs and lacewings.
- Rosemary repels bean beetles and cabbage moths.
- Thyme repels whiteflies.

my soups and casseroles, as well as for health-supportive teas and tinctures, but nettles also provide nutrition for the soil. (Wear gloves when you handle fresh nettles, which can sting when they come in contact with the skin.) Nettles will act as a companion to fruit trees when planted nearby, helping to supply good nutrition to the soil. Comfrey exhibits similar behavior. Both of these herbs work by supplying nitrogen and minerals to the soil, whether they're growing in the ground near other plants or being added to the garden soil as compost. They serve as activators in my compost barrel too, so I am sure to add chopped up nettles and comfrey leaves to the compost barrel on a regular basis during the gardening season.

Activator Tea for the Compost Pile

This brew will be great to trigger and feed the microorganisms that turn garden trimmings and kitchen vegetable waste into healthy compost. It will provide great starter nutrients to the compost. Wear gloves if you use fresh nettles; dried nettles don't sting.

Into a 5-gallon container with a lid, put the following ingredients:
- 12 cups fresh or 6 cups dried nettles, coarsely chopped
- 12 cups fresh or 6 cups dried comfrey leaves, coarsely chopped
- 2 cups kelp (flaked or powdered) or other seaweed
- 1 cup pelletized alfalfa (rabbit-feed pellets)

Once all the ingredients are in the container, fill it to within 3 inches from the rim with water. Place the lid loosely on top of the container so that some air can penetrate but the contents are protected from spilling. Allow the mixture to steep in a warm place for 4 to 8 hours. After the steeping step is complete, simply pour the entire contents of the container over the compost pile or into the compost barrel. If you are using a compost barrel, remember to rotate it a couple of turns after you secure the lid, and then vent the barrel. Your compost pile or barrel now has everything it needs to begin producing nutritious compost for the garden.

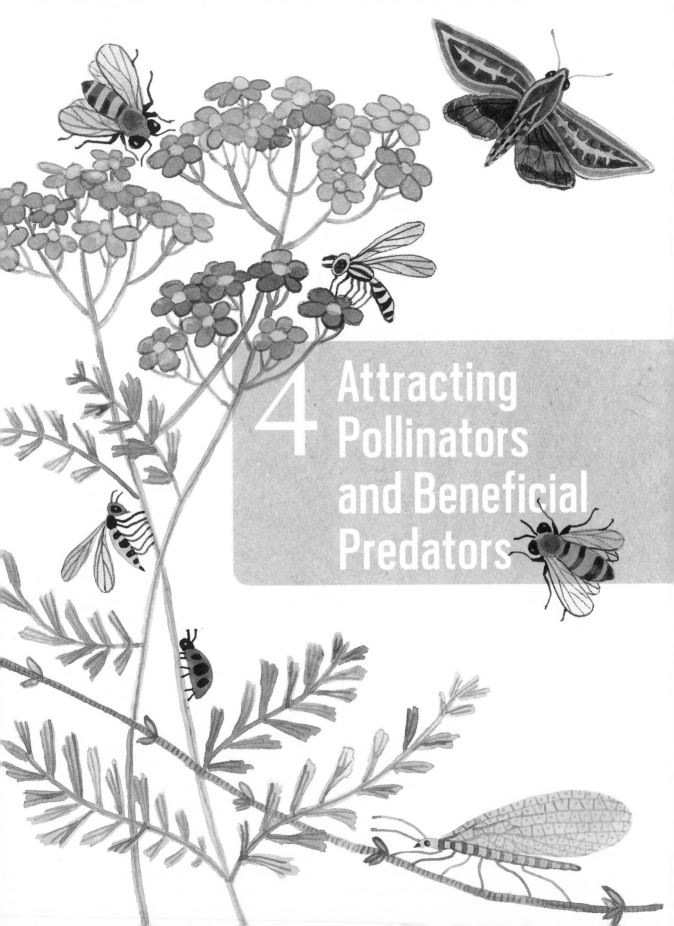

4 Attracting Pollinators and Beneficial Predators

POLLINATORS ARE CRITICALLY IMPORTANT to a successful food garden, perhaps the most important things after water, soil, and sunshine. Whereas some plants are pollinated by the wind and a few are self-pollinating, the vast majority of food plants would not survive, much less produce fruit, without the assistance of pollinating creatures. Walking through a grocery would take about 30 seconds because the shelves would be empty. Pollinators are often underappreciated, and many people are unaware of their importance to home gardens, much less to the food supply.

Pollinators are only one group of creatures that can help increase yields and improve the health of the garden. Predatory insects and spiders hold an equal position of importance for increasing the bounty of food gardens. These creatures help control pests by hunting them. Some important predators, such as wasps, do double duty as pollinators. By taking advantage of predators, you will have little or no need to fall back on pest-killing chemicals, organic or otherwise.

The most important thing you can do to foster beneficial creatures in your garden is to refrain from using pesticides. Pesticides, even organic ones, kill pollinators and beneficial predators as well as pests. By wiping out the good along with the bad, you may get a backlash as the pests rebound when their natural controls are absent. An added advantage to natural predators is that the target pest population cannot develop resistance to being hunted, as it does with pesticides. I encourage you to work with the natural cycles in the garden and let the beneficial creatures do their job before applying a pesticide. (And when you do choose a pesticide, make it an organic one — discussed later in this chapter.)

The needs of pollinators and beneficial predators are similar, and simple. Aside from an environment free of poisons, they need food, shelter, and nesting sites. To attract a wide variety of species, grow a wide variety of food for them — vegetables, fruits, nuts, herbs, flowers that bloom at different times, and native plants. *Shelter* means protection from winds and a spot to overwinter, perhaps a hedgerow or a wild patch in the corner of the yard. Nesting requirements differ greatly: some creatures lay eggs on plants, others in the ground, in hollow stems, or in dead trees. A varied landscape is aesthetically pleasing as well as welcoming.

Meet the Pollinators

Though most people think of bees when it comes to pollination, the range of creatures involved in this process is surprising. It includes different types of bees, both foreign and native, but also butterflies and moths. Even insects often seen as troublemakers — houseflies, some beetles, and

mining bee

polyester bee

cuckoo bee

cactus bee

sweat bee

carpenter bee

honeybees

mason bee

bumblebee

If they feel their nest or hive is being threatened, honeybees and bumblebees may sting, whereas most solitary bees will simply move away from their nest instead.

wasps — contribute to pollinating the fruit and vegetable garden. You'd be surprised at how many delicious fruits are pollinated by different kinds of flies. Hummingbirds pollinate many plants with tubular flowers, including many wildflowers. They're drawn to bright colors, especially reds and hot pinks. Hummingbirds have no sense of smell, so fragrance in flowers is unimportant to them. Bats pollinate some night-blooming plants with large, fragrant flowers, such as some types of passionflowers and agaves; they are also essential pollinators for several tropical fruits, among them mangoes, bananas, and guavas.

Bees

When most people think of bees, they think of bumblebees or honeybees, both good pollinators. But there are many other kinds of bees, including sweat bees, carpenter bees, digger bees, mining bees, and mason bees. Most of the latter are native species that don't sting and are just as important for pollination as bumblebees and honeybees. Wasps are also good pollinators, but since they're such good insect predators, they're discussed separately (see page 58).

Many bees don't have stingers, and those that do won't sting unless provoked. If they feel their nest or hive is being threatened, honeybees and bumblebees may sting, whereas most solitary bees will simply move away from their nest instead. If honeybees and bumblebees are out foraging for nectar and pollen, the likelihood of them stinging someone is pretty slim, as they'll be far too focused on gathering food to worry about humans. However, if accidentally bumped or grabbed by an unknowing gardener picking vegetables or fruit, they may sting. Unlike some other species that retain their stingers, honeybees do leave behind their stingers in the skin (only the females; males do not have stingers).

A stinger should be gently removed as quickly as possible using a clean, flat, dull object (such as your fingernail) to scrape it away. If you don't remove the stinger, it will continue to pump venom into your body. Most bee stings are uncomfortable but not serious — you can apply ice or a plantain poultice (see page 60) to help reduce the swelling and pain. Some folks are allergic to bee stings, and may have an allergic reaction such as nausea, vomiting, faintness, or abdominal pain. In rare cases, someone is severely allergic enough to go into anaphylactic shock. If you're allergic to bee stings and experience any of these symptoms, seek medical attention quickly.

North America has almost 4,000 species of native bees, all of which are excellent pollinators. Many live solitary lives, and the female creates a nest for her eggs in all sorts of interesting places. Female solitary bees gather pollen to feed their brood (eggs and growing larvae), as well as nectar to feed themselves. The nectar provides them with the great amounts of energy they need to forage, build nests, and lay eggs. The largest percentage of solitary bees, like digger bees and mining bees, build their nests in the ground. Still others prefer to make their nests in hollow stems or pieces of wood. Leafcutter bees and mason

Homes for Native Bees

Try placing a nesting box for solitary bees such as masons and leafcutters in or near the food garden. Mason bees, which are docile solitary bees that do not sting, build their nests in hollow tubes. You can visit a garden center or go online to purchase a nesting box designed for mason bees, or you can build one yourself. To build your own, start by cutting hollow bamboo canes into 6- to 8-inch lengths and bundling them securely with wire. Place them into a box, filling the box tightly with bamboo so that the canes will not shift around.

Once you have constructed the nesting box, nail it to the side of a building or hang with an eye hook on a sturdy tree branch. Before you know it, your nesting box will have permanent residents. Mason bees will lay their eggs inside the hollow cavities of the bamboo. Once all the eggs are within the nest and the bees have gathered and stored pollen, the female mason bees will seal the end with a plug of mud to protect the brood until they emerge as adult bees.

These nesting boxes, once put into place, are trouble-free until spring flowers start to bloom, about which time you should notice that all the hollow canes have been used as nests and the adults have emerged. Once this has happened, it's time to take the boxes down and replace the used canes with a fresh supply. Perform this task before the bees begin to build new nests. The timing can be a bit tricky, as you need to pay attention to see when the previously plugged end caps have been removed by emerging bees. Install the fresh canes before summer progresses along too far and the adult bees start to get serious about building new nests.

Beehives in the Food Garden

If you decide to become a beekeeper and care for a honeybee hive of your own, you'll need to consider where to place the hive in your garden or the surrounding landscape. Beehives are best placed in an area where there isn't much traffic from humans. The reason for this is twofold. First, if a hive is placed near a walking path or garden benches, there's a much greater risk of someone getting stung, which of course is never desirable. Second, bees moving in and out of the hive need to have an unobstructed flight path, sort of a bee superhighway without stop signs.

Hives are best oriented with the entrance facing south and slightly to the east, so that the rising sun brings first light into the small entrance, letting the bees know that it's time to get to work. Although it's not absolutely necessary, many veteran beekeepers in cold-climate areas advise supplying winter protection for the hives, especially from biting cold winds. This can be achieved by placing a hive a yard or so out from a hedgerow or windbreak of trees or shrubs. If some of those trees and shrubs are fruiting varieties, you'll witness a wonderful honeybee-pollination extravaganza during the blooming season.

bees are part of this group. Often these solitary creatures will remain dormant in their nest until season conditions are right and flowers begin to bloom. The adult bees emerge from the nest and start the life cycle all over again.

Some solitary bees, such as bumblebees, travel for more than a mile in search of nectar and pollen, while others, such as the tiny *Perdita* mining bees, travel only a couple of hundred feet. These bees forage on all different types of flowers, from daisy-shaped blossoms like coneflowers and gaillardias to tubular-shaped ones like lavenders and penstemons.

Bumblebees are able to work in cold temperatures when honeybees are still huddled in their hives. (Honeybees don't fly from a hive until the temperature is at least 50°F.) For this reason, bumblebees can be particularly helpful in early spring and late fall, and for high-altitude gardens when flowers may be blooming but it's still too chilly for the honeybees to venture out. Bumblebees frequently build nests in deserted mouse nests and other hollow burrows, often underground, but sometimes even in deserted bird nests. Bumblebees are important pollinators, especially for tomatoes and squash-family plants, such as cucumbers, squash, and gourds. They are also very helpful for pollinating many types of herbs — lavender, oregano, and basil, for example.

Bumblebees are attracted to blue flowers. Apparently they can't see red or ultraviolet-reflecting white, but they can see blue and all the other colors humans see. Bumblebees use flower color as a memory trigger to remind them which flowers have the most nectar and pollen, and where they are located. Then they return to the same flowers over and over to gather as much pollen and nectar as possible with the greatest efficiency and the least amount of energy. It's amazing that a bumblebee's sight is five times faster than a human's, which allows them to fly really fast in search of those identified flower patches. They also seek out flowers by size and contrasting color patterns.

All three factors help speed the bumblebee's search for flowers to forage on, which is important due to the amount of energy they must expend in the process.

Honeybees

Unlike solitary bees, honeybees are social and live in large colonies. They are not native to North America; they arrived in the 1600s, brought on ships by early colonists from Europe. Honeybees live in hives, sharing the work for the good of all. In a honeybee colony, most of the bees are female worker bees. There are only a few male drone bees, whose sole purpose is to mate with the queen. The one and only queen lays eggs as her primary responsibility. The female worker bees have designated tasks: maintaining the hive, guarding the hive and the queen, caring for the brood, or gathering food in the form of nectar or pollen. Honeybees typically travel up to 3 miles to forage for pollen and nectar but will go as far as 6 miles if necessary.

Honeybees are especially helpful pollinators in the food garden. They are a perfect match for many fruits and vegetables that have their origins on the European continent, such as almonds, melons, and fruit trees in the citrus, apple, and plum families. Honeybees evolved with these food plants, so they pollinate them more efficiently than they do some other plants. We notice that honeybees here on our farm sometimes cheat when it comes to pollinating certain tubular flowers, such as penstemons. Instead of crawling into the flower to get to the pollen and nectar, they simply bite a hole in the side of a flower to sip the nectar out. When they do this, no pollination of the flower happens and the development of fruit (seeds) does not occur. Still, honeybees do a great deal more pollination good than harm, and having them nearby is a wise idea for food gardeners, especially those with lots of berry bushes or fruit trees.

Your garden may have room to include a beehive or two tucked into an out-of-the-way corner. Since honeybees travel for miles to gather nectar and pollen, they may even come to your garden from hives kept by someone in your neighborhood. Thus, your neighbor's bees will benefit from your flowering trees and shrubs.

Flies That Pollinate

If you examine flowers, you'll notice that many visitors aren't bees or wasps but instead are flies. Not all flies are good pollinators, but many feed on nectar and carry pollen from flower to flower as they go on to the next meal. Flies come in many varieties. Often you have to look closely to tell whether something is a bee or a fly. Look at the eyes: those of flies are usually very large and almost meet in the middle; those of bees are off to the side. Flies usually aren't as hairy as bees (wasps aren't hairy either). Technically, flies have only two wings, while bees and wasps have four, but this can be hard to see! Bees have structures on their back legs or belly that enable them to carry pollen, a protein-rich component of their diet. So if you see bright yellow balls of pollen on the back legs, you're looking at a bee, not a fly.

Flies do not have a way to actively gather pollen, but they are avid nectar drinkers, and as they move on the flowers to get the nectar, pollen grains stick to their bodies and end up getting moved about, often pollinating the flowers in the process. Thus, though they do not intentionally pollinate flowers, they do enough pollination as

they go along to be a great help to the gardener, especially for vegetables such as carrots and onions. For gardeners who want to save their own seeds from one year to the next, the work of pollinating flies is crucial, since most bees are not interested in the flowers of root vegetables.

Some of the most important fly pollinators are hoverflies (also called flower flies or syrphid flies) and bee flies. Even the annoying housefly helps out in this process. You may see ordinary houseflies on yarrow flowers, and they're valued in the production of carrot seeds.

Hoverflies are quite beautiful, with bands of yellow, orange, and green. This colorful patterning confuses predators into thinking they are bees or wasps that can sting, though they have no stingers. They gather tiny droplets of nectar that sit on the tops of flowers of strawberry, carrot, and mustard-family plants such as broccoli and radishes. In the process of foraging for this nectar, they pollinate the flowers. Because of this, hoverflies are much valued by vegetable-seed producers. An exceptional trait of hoverflies is that they are not bothered by cold temperatures, making them helpful pollinators for high-elevation gardeners.

Butterflies and Moths

Many gardeners welcome butterflies for their beauty, but these familiar insects are also great pollinators. Although many gardeners worry when they see caterpillars on their plants, it is worth the reminder that caterpillars will lead to butterflies. Butterflies lay eggs on the foliage of some plants; when the caterpillars hatch, they feed on that same foliage. If you want to see butterflies, you must plant enough to share with the caterpillars.

Butterflies and moths are often attracted to flowers that are similar in color to themselves, offering them some camouflage protection against

What's a Butterfly House?

Butterfly houses look similar on the outside to birdhouses, except instead of having a round entry door, they have slots cut into the front panel. The slots, ½ inch wide and about 3¼ inches long, are sized to prevent entry by birds or other predators and to accommodate the way butterflies move into protected places. Slanted roofs keep butterflies inside nice and dry during rain showers. Inside the box are chunks of bark or sturdy branches screwed to the walls in upright positions that allow the butterflies to perch and rest. The houses are brightly colored, usually in shades of red, yellow, or pink, to attract the butterflies. Only untreated lumber and nontoxic paints can be used, and only the outside of the house is painted, because butterflies are very sensitive to chemical smells. You can purchase a butterfly house at a garden center or online.

A butterfly house should be mounted on a pole about 4 to 6 feet tall. It should be placed in a sunny part of the garden where there are lots of blooming perennials or shrubs like purple coneflower and butterfly bush. It is helpful if there is a water source somewhere nearby; a shallow dish of glazed pottery or glass works well as a butterfly drinking dish. Situate the butterfly house away from access by curious pets and children so that the fluttery creatures will not be disturbed.

Twice a year, in early spring and late fall, the butterfly house will benefit from being cleaned. Use a toothbrush to gently clean away any debris such as old spiderwebs, small pieces of plants that may have blown into the slots and gotten stuck there, or insect excrement.

predators. Butterflies prefer to land on flowers with flattish tops; thus, the herbs in the carrot family attract butterflies with their large, flat flower clusters. In this group of herbs are parsley, dill, cilantro (coriander), cumin, fennel, and celery. Oregano is a good nectar plant for several types of butterfly. On flowers with long throats, like buddleias (butterfly bush), butterflies unroll their long tongues to get to the nectar deep within.

Many garden flowers — among them cosmos, marigolds, phlox, salvias, and sedums — attract butterflies by supplying nectar. Others that serve as host plants include asters and daisies, butterfly weed, joe-pye weed, and lupines. These make attractive additions to beds and borders near the food garden. (If you grow them with your food plants, be aware that these flowers are not edible.) You can guess how butterfly bush gets its name, and glossy abelia (*Abelia × grandiflora*) is another shrub that's covered with butterflies when it's in bloom. It's easy to incorporate these shrubs in a hedgerow or as part of a windbreak near the food garden.

Moths are fascinating because many work the night shift: they do their pollinating between dusk and dawn. Some examples of night-blooming plants are many species of evening primrose, night-blooming cereus, and blazing star (*Mentzelia*). Other plants keep their flowers open both night and day, maximizing their pollination success. Some examples are certain cacti, some yuccas, most species of agave (except century plants, which are pollinated by bats), scarlet gaura, four o'clocks (*Mirabilis multiflora* and *M. longiflora*), hawthorn trees, some shrubby potentillas, almost all eriogonums, and anise hyssop and other *Agastache* species.

Because birds often eat butterflies and moths, plants that attract birds should be placed in a different area of the garden from those that lure butterflies and moths. However, some perennial flowers attract both birds and butterflies; among these are goldenrods (*Solidago* spp.), black-eyed Susans (*Rudbeckia* spp.), and Mexican hat coneflower (*Ratibida columnifera*). Butterflies are drawn to these in the flowering stage when they are full of sweet nectar. After the flowers have gone to seed and butterflies are no longer interested in them, the seed-eating birds like goldfinches will flock to them in droves.

Meet the Beneficial Predators

Beneficial predators manage pests that seem to come to every vegetable garden at some point during the growing season, so a wise gardener makes them welcome. Each type has its favorite prey, so it is quite important to encourage a diverse community of them in the garden space. These "good bugs" consist of both insects and spiders (which are arachnids, not insects). Before you can welcome predators into the garden, you must be able to recognize which are helpful and good and which are pests. Once you can distinguish which bugs you want to encourage, and which you do not want wreaking havoc, you can begin to welcome the beneficial ones to help you eradicate the pests.

Gallery of Beneficial Predators

A lady beetle larva will eat 25 aphids a day and the adult lady beetle will eat as many as 60. Both adults and larvae feed on soft-bodied pests, such as caterpillars as well as aphids. Most adults have bright-colored wing shells that are orange, yellow, or red with black spots, but some have black shells with orange spots. The larvae look totally unlike beetles — they have black elongated bodies with yellow or orange markings on them.

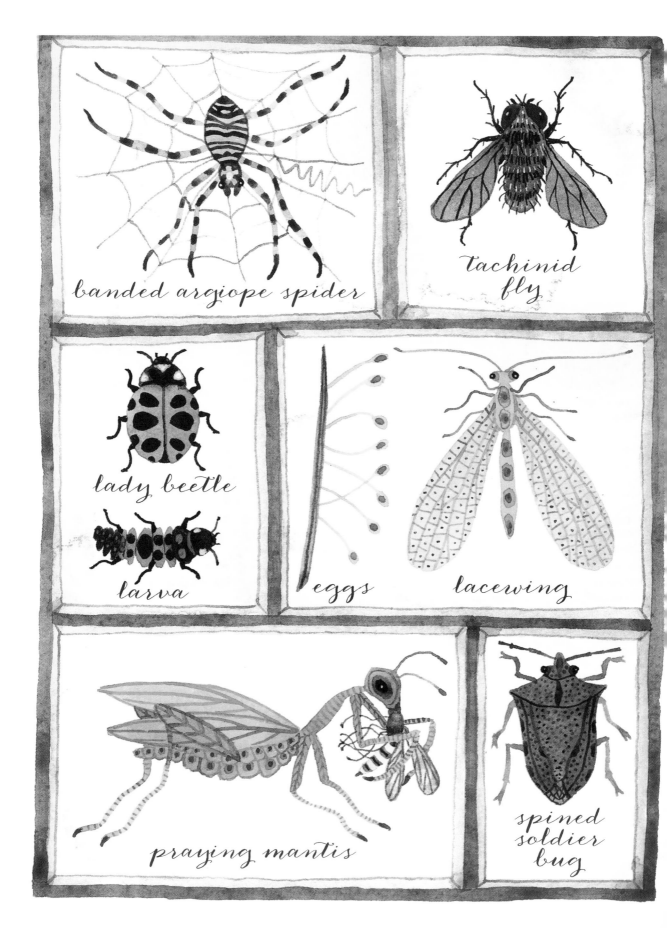

banded argiope spider

tachinid
fly

lady beetle

larva

eggs

lacewing

praying mantis

spined
soldier
bug

Adult lacewings are lovely creatures with translucent, sparkling wings on green or brown bodies. Green lacewings frequent gardens, whereas their brown cousins prefer more cover and tend to live in trees and shrubs. Lacewing larvae, sometimes called aphid lions, have hooked jaws and look a bit like alligators. They are aggressive hunters of many pests, including aphids, mites, and leafhoppers. Green lacewing eggs are easy to recognize; laid individually or in clusters, they have a silken, threadlike stalk that attaches them to a plant.

Spined soldier bugs look like their relatives the stinkbugs, having that same armor-type shell. They produce the same disagreeable odor if crushed. Unlike pest stinkbugs, spined soldier bugs mostly eat caterpillars, by stabbing them with their sucking mouthparts. They are common in gardens and very beneficial.

Tachinid flies look a bit like the common housefly, only slightly larger. These parasitic flies lay their eggs on or in the soft-bodied larvae of earwigs, caterpillars, beetles, and grasshoppers. When the eggs hatch, the larvae devour their host. A few species of tachinid flies lay their eggs on plant leaves, hatching inside the host insect after it has unknowingly eaten the eggs while munching on the leaves of the plant.

Praying Mantises

A familiar predator in the garden is the praying mantis, which gets its name because while hunting it holds up its front legs as though praying. This insect comes in green and brown and sort of resembles a twig, except that this twig moves and has large eyes on the outside edges of its head. Mantises often occur naturally in the garden, hatching in spring from an inch-wide egg sac that overwinters among perennial plants. (A good reason not to trim back and tidy up perennials in the garden until later in the spring is that these plants provide good habitat for many beneficial insects as well as seeds for wild birds.) These insects hatch out as tiny beasts about ¼ inch long, but reach 2 to 4 inches when fully mature. They are cute as anything, especially when they're tiny. Not shy around humans, they're fairly easy to watch while working in the garden. Despite being cute, they are ferocious hunters of insects. Unfortunately they eat any insect they can catch, including beneficial insects and pollinators. They also cannibalize each other, especially when they're small, until only a few are left within the boundaries of even a large garden landscape. Famously, the female often does in the male after she has mated with him.

Praying mantises are large enough to take on big insects such as grasshoppers and crickets. Because grasshoppers can quickly devour plants in the garden, I welcome the one or two praying mantises that make their home in mine. Occasionally, we come across one that has found its way into a greenhouse; the praying mantis earns its comfy home in there by helping with greenhouse pest management. You can purchase praying mantis egg sacs in the spring, but it's usually best not to encourage a huge population. It is likely you have a few in your garden already.

Spiders

Spiders have gotten a bad rap. The common thinking that all spiders are evil and should be squashed underfoot is simply wrong. Spiders are amazing hunters. They will patrol your garden, catching and eating all manner of insect pests. Notice how beautiful their webs are and how they sparkle when the morning dew is on them. Spiders come in any manner of colors and shapes. The common garden spiders we have are called banded argiopes and have striped legs that make them look almost comical. They sport yellow and black stripes or, less often, chartreuse and black banding. The banded argiope is a medium-sized orb weaver and is common in the western part of North America. Another helper in our garden is the monkey-faced spider (*Araneus gemmoides*), sometimes called a cat-face or humpback spider. It's a sort of a peachy tan, with two orange spots on the back end of its abdomen on the underside. If you look up at this spider in its web, you may see what looks like the face of a monkey or perhaps of a cat staring back down at you. The monkey-faced spider is a very large orb weaver — I measured one on the porch at 1¼ inches across at the widest part of its body. They are good fly predators and create beautiful large webs in the greenhouses and in the garden.

Other species of orb weavers are common garden helpers in other parts of the country. Yes, there are spiders you should approach with care — the black widow and the brown recluse, for example — but they are few in number. The vast majority of spiders are helpful in the garden and deserve respect.

Wasps

Wasps are valuable in the food garden. Several excel at pest patrol, and a few are important pollinators. When most people think of wasps, they think of hornets and yellow jackets. These are social wasps, and they can be annoying. But there are also many types of solitary wasps, and most of them don't sting.

Paper wasps (*Polistes* spp.) feed on caterpillars, earworms, beetles, and flies, in addition to some other insects. They can sting but usually will do so only if their papery nest is threatened in some way. Baldfaced hornets (*Dolichovespula maculata*) are tree-dwelling paper-nest wasps. They are also beneficial to gardens because they feed their young live insects, mainly caterpillars. They will also sting if their nest is threatened. Another useful wasp is the parasitizing trichogramma. This incredibly small wasp lays its eggs in the larvae of pest insects such as caterpillars, earworms, and whiteflies. When the eggs hatch, the larvae feed on the host, leaving behind only an empty shell. These very tiny wasps are especially helpful in a greenhouse.

Good Bug or Bad Bug?

Learning to identify insects and other bugs has become an ongoing task for me, and one that I'm still a long way from completing. There are a great number of bugs out there! Hardly a day passes when I'm outdoors that I don't see a new one. I depend on reference books to help me identify the beneficial bugs and understand how they work to our advantage for biological pest management in our garden landscape, in our flower seed crop production field, and in our greenhouses.

Consider investing in a handheld magnifying glass and one or two good identification books for garden bugs, both beneficial ones and pests. Choose a large magnifying lens so that you can see not only the creature you're trying to identify but also what's going on around it. Is it eating the plant, laying eggs, or eating a pest? You can find good reference books, as well as a couple of websites to help with identification, in the Resources section at the end of this book.

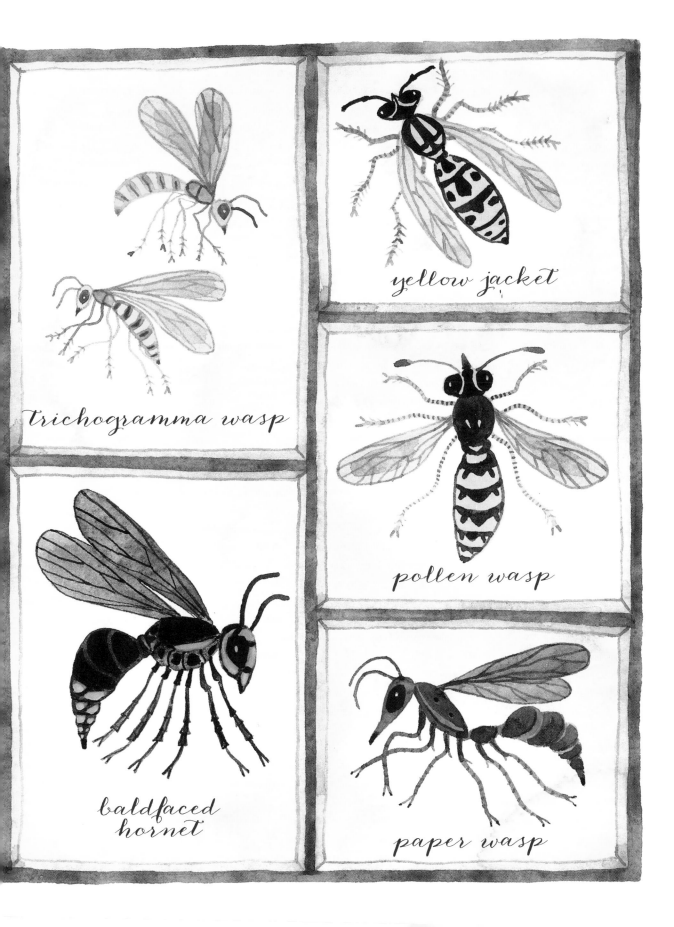

trichogramma wasp

yellow jacket

pollen wasp

baldfaced
hornet

paper wasp

Some wasps can be useful pollinators, although they're not as efficient at this task as bees are. Most wasps feed on nectar only as adults in need of quick nourishment to transform into energy. These small solitary wasps are pretty, gentle creatures as they move around and through the flowers. They prefer those that are shallow-throated like those of fennel and members of the carrot family, such as carrots, parsley, and celery. They also pollinate garden flowers, among them goldenrod and butterfly weed. Pollen wasps (*Pseudomasaris* spp.) are the only wasps that actually collect nectar and pollen and take them back to the nest to feed their young.

For the most part, hornets and yellow jackets don't bother anyone and simply conduct their business of foraging for insects or nectar and pollinating the flowers as they go. There are, however, some places where stinging insects are not welcome: right by a door or a table on a porch are two examples. In these cases, it's best to remove a nest and look for ways to lure the wasps elsewhere.

Soothe Stings with a Plantain Poultice

When pollinators are intent on their task of gathering nectar or pollen, they generally have little time or interest for people gardening in the same area. If you get stung or bitten by an insect or a spider, you can easily make yourself a soothing plantain poultice that will help relieve the pain, swelling, and itchiness. Plantain is a common weed in most lawns, so you probably have some close at hand. There are two kinds of common plantain: English or narrow-leaf plantain (*Plantago lanceolata*) and broadleaf or anasazi plantain (*Plantago major*). Either will work nicely. You can confirm that you have the correct plant when you find what you think is plantain by gently pulling on a leaf lengthwise. It will tear apart and as it does so, it will have little white elastic cords that run through it. This is your clue.

Start by harvesting one whole plantain plant, roots and all. Wash off any lingering soil. Fill a 2-quart pan half full of water and set over high heat. Coarsely chop the plantain. Once the water boils, add the chopped plant to the pan, reducing the heat so that the water goes to a gentle simmer. Allow the plantain to simmer for about 5 minutes, then turn off the heat, cover the pan, and steep for another 5 minutes.

Put ¼ to ½ cup of simmered plantain in the center of a clean washcloth or cloth napkin. Use string or a thick rubber band to tie it into a bundle. Check to make sure the poultice is warm, but not so hot it would burn skin. Hold the poultice on the skin over the sting or bite for a minimum of 20 minutes.

Then remove the poultice and discard into the compost pile. Never reuse a poultice, and always launder the cloth before using it again. You can store any unused poultice in a covered container in the refrigerator for up to 48 hours, in case you want a second application for a severe sting. Just reheat the poultice, put it in a clean cloth, and hold it on the bite as before.

Good Plants for Pollinators and Beneficial Predators

Many so-called weeds are wonderful fodder for both pollinators and predators, making it wise to practice a degree of tolerance when it comes to weed management, to maximize the variety and numbers of pollinators that will visit the garden. Some of these same weeds can provide food for humans as well. Take the notorious dandelion. You can use the tender leaves in spring as salad greens. Once they bloom, you can mix the yellow flowers with some minced onion, flour, and seasoning herbs and fry them up as dandelion fritters. You can also gather a large amount of the flower heads for dandelion wine. The chopped and roasted roots of dandelion can be used as a coffee substitute, much like those of chicory, a common roadside weed with beautiful blue flowers. Another edible weed is common purslane: large-leaved forms are a nice addition to salad mixes and are an excellent source of healthful omega-3 fatty acids.

Planting a variety of herbs in and around the food garden helps create a welcoming environment for pollinators and other beneficial insects, such as lady beetles, lacewings, moths, and butterflies. Chamomile attracts beneficial wasps and hoverflies. The large leaves of horseradish provide shelter for beneficial insects and spiders, and the plant may act as a decoy to lure grasshoppers away from other plants. When thyme is in bloom, it's often covered with honeybees; have a good look before you harvest a handful of thyme to be sure you're not grabbing a bee at the same time! Oregano and lemon balm are also wonderful for honeybees. Herbs add beauty to the garden and flavor to the kitchen.

Herbs typically are quite aromatic. They contain volatile oils, which supply their wonderful fragrances and flavors, even some medicinal properties. Many of those same aromatic oils act as deterrents to pests in the garden; mice are not crazy about the smell of strong mint, and deer usually avoid sage and lavender.

The wise gardener will grow many flowers around and inside the food garden to attract not only pollinators but also beneficial predators. Pest insects are often attracted to flowering plants that are highly fragrant — for example, sweet alyssum and other members of the mustard family. Have you ever noticed how sweet-smelling the flowers of arugula and radishes are? This is one of the reasons they can become infested with aphids or flea beetles. Predatory insects know that sweet-smelling flowers may be the perfect place to find dinner. The predators often lay their eggs on flowering plants such as yarrow and chamomile so that when the eggs hatch, the larvae will have

Coexisting with Wasps

I know wasps are valuable pollinators because I see them all over the fennel flowers nearly every day that the fennel is blooming. While I admit it's taken me a number of years to develop my comfort level around them, I've learned to redirect wasps away from places where it's not a good idea for them to be. I discourage them from building their nests in my clothesline poles by duct-taping the ends of the poles. Without an easy entry door, they go elsewhere to build their nest. If we're having trouble with wasps wanting to linger over our dinner plates, I hang a pint-size canning jar half full of honey water in a tree far away from the back porch. They are lured away by the sweet water.

Strategically incorporating annuals and perennials in and around the food garden will assist you in pest control — and you'll have the wonderful added advantage of the colorful beauty these flowers bring.

a good supply of pest insects, as well as some nectar, to feed on.

Strategically incorporating annuals and perennials in and around the food garden will assist you in pest control — and you'll have the delightful added advantage of the color these flowers bring. Aphids are drawn to plants like marigolds, roses, chamomile, and angelica, so you'll see plenty of lady beetles in all stages of their life cycle on the leaves and flowers of these same plants feasting on aphids. Cosmos — cheerful annuals that add bright shades of pink, red, and white to the garden — attract spined soldier bugs, which are good predators of caterpillars and beetle larvae, such as of the Colorado potato beetle. I love the delicate lacy scabiosa, sometimes called pincushion plant. Scabiosa flowers provide great fodder for honeybees and

also attract hoverflies, whose larvae forage on the aphids that may be lingering in that part of the garden. Design your garden so that you have some of these flowering plants close to your fruits and vegetables.

Organic Pesticides: Only as a Last Resort!

Sometimes even in a healthy garden, a pest population will explode. If you decide there is no alternative to using a pesticide, choose the least toxic organic one that will do the job. Remember that even organic pesticides will kill beneficial insects and pollinators along with pests, which is never a good thing. Organic pesticides, like all other ones, require careful handling to prevent skin irritation, and some, such as pyrethrum, can be toxic to pets and people if not used correctly. Some can make birds sick. The first step in applying an organic pesticide is to read the label thoroughly! Wear gloves and long sleeves, long pants, and shoes to lessen the possibility of contact with the skin, which may cause irritation. Shower off and wash your clothes immediately after you apply any pesticide.

Check the label to make sure the product is effective against the target pest or disease. Look for an Organic Materials Review Institute (OMRI) registration or the US Department of Agriculture (USDA) organic logo to make sure it is safe for organic gardens and the environment at large. Follow the label instructions to the letter. Applying pesticides inappropriately or too often not only will harm beneficial insects but also may create resistance in the pest population you are targeting. Inappropriate application may also harm the plants you are trying to save. For example, summer oil (horticultural oil) will burn plants if applied in hot, sunny weather; peppers

A Dozen Aromatic Herbs for Welcoming Beneficials

- Anise hyssop
- Basil
- Chamomile
- Dill
- Lavender
- Lemon balm
- Lemon verbena
- Mint, especially peppermint and spearmint
- Oregano
- Rosemary
- Sage
- Thyme

and basil seem to be very susceptible to being burned, so wait until late in the day, when temperatures cool off, to spray them.

Pollinators, including honeybees, are extremely sensitive to chemicals of all types. Wait to apply pesticides until after dusk, when honeybees have gone home to their hives and are no longer foraging on the flowers. Choose, too, a calm evening when no rain is expected. Even a gentle breeze can carry pesticide drift to unintended areas. Target or spot-treat only where the pest problem exists.

Pesticides, organic or otherwise, should not be applied near or over ponds, ditches, streams, container fountains, or other water sources.

Many formulas are highly toxic to fish, turtles, salamanders, and other aquatic organisms. Water often carries pesticides to unintended areas of the landscape, or even into the greater environment. There are few, but important, exceptions to this rule. A special formulation of *Bt* (*Bacillus thuringiensis* subsp. *israelensis*) that affects only mosquito larvae is an excellent tool, especially for gardens that contain a pond, fountain, or rain barrel. This biological larvicide is applied directly to standing water in containers. Killing off the larvae helps reduce the mosquito population, thus helping prevent the spread of diseases such as the West Nile virus.

5 Creating Habitats for Wildlife

ENCOURAGING WILDLIFE TO TAKE UP RESIDENCE, thrive, and help increase the harvest in your garden requires thinking about how to accommodate animals' needs as well as your own. In other words, you have to think about habitat.

Habitat, of course, doesn't just mean providing a place for critters to live; it also means allowing their natural cycles of interdependence to carry on. Mice will come into gardens to forage on fruit and seeds. No need to put out mouse poison, though, because the mice provide food for hawks and garter or bull snakes. Those same hawks and snakes also eat grasshoppers and crickets and other large insects. And when the mice have deserted their nests, bumblebees will often take them over for their own use. Since bumblebees are important pollinators, especially for cucumbers, squash, and gourds, not to mention all those delicious homegrown tomatoes, I'm certainly happy for them to settle in.

Coexistence occurs on different levels. The simplest level is avoiding harm without trying in order to foster wildlife as a contributing partner to the gardening experience. You may simply welcome wild creatures with no significant action on your part and enjoy the benefits they bring to the garden. Bird-watchers may list all the birds they see in their gardens without noticing which ones are foraging on which insects. You might notice a sudden population of baby toads hopping around without connecting it to the disappearance of the slugs that were pestering the strawberry bed a week or so earlier.

The next level is paying close attention to the goings-on in the garden to determine not only what wildlife is there but also the relationships among plants and animals and pests. As you become more observant, you'll notice what the various creatures are doing.

Close observation is also required for the highest level of coexistence: actively fostering wildlife amid the plant world so as to benefit all. This is the kind of wildlife gardening I find to be most inspiring. Though it is not without challenges, the benefits for all concerned outweigh the problems.

Actively fostering complex communities means enhancing gardens to make them better ecosystems. There are quite a few ways you can go about this task. The simplest way is to notice what is already going on in a garden and support it. For example, if you notice a particular bird, research its food preferences and nesting habits. Perhaps you can enhance its diet by planting a particular shrub. Or you may be able to enhance nesting sites; to encourage bluebirds, for example, purchase a birdhouse designed for bluebirds and install it at the edge of a field. Some other forms of active partnership are creating habitats by planting hedgerows or herbs and flowers, installing feeding stations, adding homes such as bat houses, and providing water sources such as birdbaths.

Welcome Animal Predators

Predators such as toads, nonpoisonous snakes, foxes, owls, and hawks can be amazing allies. These hunters help manage troublesome critters that come into the food garden to eat things we don't want them to eat or to dig around and damage roots. Without such hunters, gardens would have too many plant-eating critters like cottontail rabbits and gophers. All wildlife populations remain in better proportion to one another and to the habitat that sustains them if there are checks and balances, hunters and prey. Give the hunters access to the areas in and around a garden and you will be pleased to see that its landscape can benefit from their presence.

Build animal predators a home or offer them a habitat so that they can build their own in or near the garden. As long as there's hunting to be done, they'll be on the job. You may hear them on a summer's night through an open window as they go about their work. Set up a wildlife camera in the garden to catch sight of these helpers. They are majestic and beautiful creatures worthy of your appreciation and respect.

Birds, bats, beneficial insects, and even fish may eat twice their own weight in pest insects in a day. They will devour aphids, mosquitoes, and squash bugs. Many of these predators benefit a garden in other ways, such as by pollinating flowers and by supplying fertilizer from their waste.

Bats deserve respect and admiration. They fly through the night sky using echolocation to home in on flying insects. North American bats aren't bloodsuckers. What they eat are mosquitoes — lots and lots of them — along with other night-flying insects. Bats also pollinate some night-blooming flowers. It is true that bats occasionally carry rabies, just as some other wild animals occasionally do. (If you come across a bat or any other wild animal lying on the ground or behaving strangely, assume it is sick and call the local wildlife control officer.) The numbers are small, however; fewer than 20 cases in a decade according to the Centers for Disease Control. So, given the many thousands of bats out there helping manage insect populations and pollinating plants, they are always welcome in my garden landscape.

Toads and frogs eat more than just mosquitoes and crickets. They also feast on slugs and pill bugs. We have bullfrogs in our pond, and I was startled to see one with a mouse in its mouth, but then I learned that bullfrogs eat all sorts of creatures, not just insects and small fish. Nonpoisonous snakes like garter snakes and bull snakes feed on insects, but they also hunt mice and voles.

A few rodents in the vegetable garden is nothing to worry about, but if their numbers get too high, you may dig up a lot of partially eaten

Bodacious Bug-Eaters

Welcoming wild birds and domestic chickens or turkeys into the garden can be a wonderful management tool for squash bugs, grasshoppers, Colorado potato beetles, flea beetles, and other hard-bodied pest insects. Red-winged blackbirds go on a feeding frenzy once their nesting season is over, and the timing of this massive feeding event is right in line with when these types of pest insects really get their population numbers up. Fortunately for us, our ponds are prime nesting grounds for the red-wings, and we have plenty of these birds in the neighborhood to take care of our beetle and hopper insects, as well as squash bugs, before they become problems.

Help from a Hawk

A sharp-shinned hawk and her mate live in our large old mulberry tree from late autumn through spring. (During the summer they migrate.) She's very beautiful, and he's quite a handsome bird. The first time I saw her down on the ground in the bird garden, running back and forth among the bushes, I thought something was terribly wrong. Not often have I seen a hawk on the ground, much less dashing around helter-skelter. Then I realized what she was doing — she was after a mouse, which she caught.

Another time, I saw her mate catch a Eurasian collared dove in flight. Eurasian collared doves are an invasive species; in North America their populations have spread with unbelievable speed in recent years. They often drive away native birds such as mourning doves, eating their food sources and displacing them from nesting habitat. We have a lot of them here on the farm, and I'm quite happy that the hawks find them a tasty meal. Now that the hawks are hunting the collared doves, which are slower and not so savvy, mourning doves are returning. Hawks, like other predators, hold a critical place in nature, helping take care of problems and keeping things in balance.

potatoes or carrots, or find significant damage from their burrowing. Hawks, falcons, owls, and other birds of prey are proficient when it comes to managing populations of mice, rabbits, and squirrels. Other great helpers in this department are foxes, coyotes, and bobcats, all of which are becoming more common in suburbia. These animals are often around even if people don't realize it and never even catch a glimpse of them. Though coyotes and bobcats frighten some people, they cause little real damage and eat a lot of mice.

Problems with animal predators do arise for gardeners who allow domestic rabbits, chickens, turkeys, or small pets to roam freely, especially at night, without protection. Peaceful coexistence requires taking responsibility to be sure that pets are indoors or safely housed at night, when wild animals do most of their hunting. Domestic rabbits and fowl must be housed in secure, predator-proof hutches and coops. If you leave them unprotected, it won't be a wild animal's fault that it ate your chicken.

I have two cats, Pouncita and Gwenivere, and they dearly love to go outside and into our gardens. They are not allowed outside when we are not home to keep tabs on them. They are also not allowed outside before the sun is up and must come indoors before dusk. Chris and I pay attention as we are working and moving about on the property for signs of wild hunters, noting when we see scat, evidence of digging, or bird feathers strewn about. If we see a fox, we take note of the time of day so that we can make sure our cats are not out when the fox is making its rounds. Wild animals tend to be creatures of habit, so if a fox is moving through, chances are it will move through the next day at about the same time. When we hear the bobcat at night, the next evening we often hear it at almost exactly the same time. We have great horned owls and bald eagles in the area, both of which could carry off a small dog or cat. If we see these birds of prey or hear their calls, we keep Pouncita and Gwenivere in for a few days just to be safe. The sharp-shinned hawk we often see is no threat to the cats because she and her mate hunt smaller prey.

If you see wild hunters, or signs of them, in your garden landscape, take time to learn a little bit about them. Research what they hunt and what time of the day they typically move about; you will be better prepared to take care of your domestic animals accordingly. Really, when you think about it, it's not so much different from protecting your domestic animals from other threats such as being hit by a car or attacked by a stray dog.

Wild animals need three primary things to begin to make a habitat a home. First, they need a source of water. Second, they need one or more sources of food. These can come in the way of naturally existing food supplies, such as seed heads and existing wildlife (for example, slugs supply food to toads and salamanders). Food supplies may be supplemented with, for example, bird feeders. The third need is shelter. This includes safety from predators and possibly a place to raise young that is protected from the elements. To create attractive habitats to bring wildlife into your garden, you must ensure that each component is available to provide for these primary needs. Let's look at each one in more detail.

Supply Water Sources

Perhaps you are fortunate enough to have a naturally occurring water source near your garden, such as a stream or creek that runs through your property. Maybe your garden sits on the shoreline of a lake. If so, the work of providing a source of fresh water for wildlife is already done for you. Regardless of whether your water source is natural or human-made, it can be a beautiful, practical, and fun part of your garden.

Without an existing source, providing a water supply could be as simple as placing a birdbath in the part of the garden where you hope to attract birds. Birds will use this for drinking as well as for bathing. Bathing helps birds keep their feathers clean and keep cool during the hot season. If possible, locate the birdbath where you can see it as you sit by a window or on the back porch. Watching them in action draws you in so that you can hardly make yourself stop. It's a great way to learn more about their habits. Who in the bird community gets along and who does not? What is their daily routine? Watch them gather on the edges to get a drink, or plunge in to splash and bathe.

Birdbaths

You'll need to make a commitment to fill the birdbath with fresh water daily and to rinse it out more thoroughly every couple of days to remove debris and algae from under the water level. It's a good idea to scrub with hot soapy water and a scrub brush once a month. Rinse it several times to make sure all soap residue is gone before filling it back up. Regular cleaning is important to prevent disease from spreading within the bird community, especially when several species are using the same water supply for both drinking and bathing.

Birds can't use a deep or large birdbath without some kind of island or ladder to keep them from falling in and drowning. I have two beautiful quartz rocks I found while hiking that I placed in the center of my birdbath bowl. These provide birds with a perfect landing spot to stand on.

Birdbaths in Winter

Freezing temperatures can leave thick ice in the birdbath. Where winter temperatures aren't too severe, keeping a beautiful stone of some size in the center of the birdbath will help prevent the water from freezing solid and cracking it. If the stone is dark-colored, it will heat up fast in the warm sunshine and help thaw the water more quickly.

In winter I fill the birdbath only partway, 2 to 3 inches below the rim, which then allows me to pour in a bucket of hot tap water first thing on cold mornings when I'm also filling the bird feeders. The hot water helps melt the ice that formed during a frigid night. Warm water to drink on very cold mornings, along with a good supply of bird food, really makes a difference in how well birds can cope with those extra-cold days.

You can invest in a heater to keep the water thawed, but be aware that these use a lot of electricity. Their cords can be hazardous to animals (wild and domestic) that may chew into them, or to humans who may trip over them. I prefer the bucket-of-hot-water method to thaw ice.

Ponds

For large yards, building a pond of some sort is another option for supplying water. Garden ponds can be elaborate or simple in design. They require some work to keep them clean and reduce the growth of algae. They might contain plants, such as water lilies and water hyacinths, or perhaps a fountain or pond bubbler. Both the water plants and the fountain or bubbler help reduce algae. We use a windmill-powered pond aerator to help keep the water clean.

A garden pond becomes a home to frogs, salamanders, turtles, and birds, in addition to fish. Larger wildlife can be attracted to the pond, too, and this may or may not be desirable. For example, it might be fine for the neighborhood fox to get a morning drink from it, but if fish also live in the pond, it may become challenging to keep raccoons or herons from going fishing in it for their dinner. See page 114 for how to keep a pond from becoming a fish buffet.

We have two ponds on our farm. The larger one sits in our orchard and is home to all manner of wildlife. There are bluegills that have come into the pond with the delivery of our irrigation water from Four Mile Creek. They earn their keep by helping to manage the mosquito population. We also have three red-eared slider turtles, a species native to Colorado, that we introduced

A garden pond becomes a
home to frogs, salamanders,
turtles, and birds,
in addition to fish.

into the pond about eight years ago. We have some wooden logs that float in the pond where the turtles like to sunbathe, so we see them almost every day of the gardening season. Turtles also eat bugs, so they're helping us manage pest insects, too.

In addition, we have a smaller, shallow pond in the middle of the greenhouse compound. This pond serves to hold our irrigation water when it is delivered until we need it for the gardens and flower-seed crops. When the pond was first built, one of our farm crew put in 10 small goldfish. In retrospect, it wasn't the best idea because the goldfish have reproduced rather abundantly. There's no way for them to get out of the pond. However, several creatures are helping keep the goldfish population within bounds.

We have a great blue heron, along with a number of other waterbirds that make our ponds a regular stopping place. Sometimes we see the heron standing in the middle of the goldfish pond enjoying a feast. Both ponds have become nesting habitat for red-winged blackbirds because native cattails and shrubby willows have colonized the banks over the years. Resident bullfrogs feed on the smaller goldfish, and the neighborhood raccoons and skunks hunt around the ponds regularly.

The ponds offer other advantages for our gardens and orchards. Mosquito larvae in the water appeal to several forms of wildlife, including bats. The birds that live around the ponds help with pest management in the gardens and fields by foraging on caterpillars, beetles, and similar pests. In addition, the water we use from the ponds for irrigation is rich in nutrients from the fish feces and bird droppings.

Provide Food Sources

The second key element for attracting wildlife is to make sure your garden space, or the surrounding area, is well endowed with abundant food sources. Providing the right food will help you retain the birds and other animals you already have and attract others; it may also satisfy pesky deer so they leave your vegetables alone. To begin this process, make a list of the various types of wildlife already in and around your yard that you want to support. Consider, too, whether there are wild creatures that might visit if you could provide a more inviting habitat and food supply for them.

Don't Be So Tidy

An easy way to provide food is to leave all the seed heads and stalks on perennial plants through the winter. The seeds offer a nutritious food supply to birds, small mammals such as squirrels and raccoons, and even deer to some extent. Plus the birds collect bits and pieces of leaves, twigs, stalks, seed-hair fluff, and so on, which they expertly weave into nests in which to raise their young.

Resist the urge to tidy up the garden in late fall. As an added benefit, the dead stalks of perennials offer protection to a plant's crown in winter, helping to shield it from the harshest winds and intense sunlight when there's no snow cover. The extra protection may also reduce winter kill. I do remove the annuals that have finished their growing season. They can harbor diseases, and I don't want them to spread unwanted seeds throughout the garden.

Chris and I love to watch the birds, so most of these little bird gardens are located where

we can see them from windows throughout the house and the back porch. However, they are more than places from which to watch the birds, even though that is quite nice. The wild birds are an integral part of our conservation and pest-management protocols both for our food gardens and for our perennial-seed crops. They are a formalized part of our USDA organic-certification plan, too. We want the birds around in abundance so that they will forage on the pests that might otherwise cause us a great deal of trouble by damaging our food plants and seed crops. By leaving the task of pest management in the beaks of the wild birds, we find that there are very few times when we have to manage pests through other measures like organic pesticides.

Provide Bird Feeders

It is lovely to put out feeders of various types to attract wild birds to your garden. I think it is possible to purchase or build bird feeders that resemble just about anything. Some even look like condominiums. We have wire-mesh tube feeders that hold Niger thistle; we also have thistle cloth socks or bags. Both are wonderful for the goldfinches and the pine siskins, which prefer to hang upside down as they are enjoying a meal. I have a large homemade platform feeder for the bigger birds that have trouble using the tube feeders and display no interest in the thistle bags. These large birds, and some of the smaller ones, like curve-billed thrashers, red-winged black birds, even the rosy house finches, prefer the feeders that dispense black oil sunflower and millet seeds. In winter I put down dishes that are for the ground-feeding birds like mourning doves and chickadees.

I have learned by experience that it is best to fill the feeders early in the morning, in part so the birds will have a full day of dining available

to them before the nocturnal animals begin their foraging. We have raccoons that visit my platform bird feeders almost every night. If I filled the feeders late in the day, the raccoons would be able to pillage them, and I have no doubt that this is exactly what they would do. As it is, by nightfall the feeders are mostly empty. This works out perfectly, because the raccoons visit and find just a little bit of millet and sunflower seeds available to them. They get enough of a snack to be satisfied, so they do not tear up other things or raid the gardens. We watch the raccoons from our kitchen window, which is 4 or 5 feet away from the platform. They know we are there, but they are courageous creatures and not easily deterred. They have their late-evening snack of seeds, and then they leave.

Alternately, you can provide birds with food sources that grow on plants from which they can forage at will. I think either way is good, and perhaps like us you will choose a combination of the two approaches. You will reap the rewards in your bird-watching pleasure and in the amount of pests the birds will take care of for you.

You can choose to provide food supplies for different types of wildlife as well. Aside from the birds and raccoons, we usually do not feed the wild animals that live around us, except by strategically planting in places where we want to encourage wildlife. They can, and do, forage from these plants on their own without being problematic to us.

Set Out Garden Discards

I occasionally put out food for wild creatures in the form of garden and orchard discards, but I'm careful that what I put out is appropriate for the types of animals I hope will eat that food. I gather up all the fruit that falls on the ground, and any squash or pumpkins that get overgrown before I realize it, along with carrot tops, the outer leaves of cabbage, and so forth. I put all of these discards under the pear tree in the front yard. The skunks and raccoons come by at night, whereas the squirrels and deer snack there during the day. Even the curve-billed thrashers pick through the offerings.

By taking the time to create a predictable spot for garden discards, I encourage the wildlife to look there for handouts. The process cleans up the garden areas at the bottom of the fruit trees and in the vegetable garden. Because there is not normally fallen fruit in the orchard or overgrown vegetables in the garden, the wild animals and birds do not spend much time looking there for something to eat.

The deer pass through our property at least twice each day to drink from the ponds and to forage on the pasture grass and hedgerow plantings as they are moving through the neighborhood. The mother deer often keep their fawns here hidden in our hedgerows the better part of each day. I believe they know it is a safe place for them. We have been in such a severe drought over the past two years that there is not much for wildlife to forage on in Colorado. These nursing deer have had a rough time getting enough nourishment to be able to raise their babies, so I have taken to putting out a ½-gallon bucket of whole dried corn each morning under the pear tree. I know the deer will be around by late morning, and the does eat the corn immediately.

The treat for me is that several sweet little fawns are frequently hanging out in the hedgerow that is just outside my studio windows. As I work, I get the privilege of watching them play and rest just a few feet away. My being there does not cause them any concern; indeed, one of the does puts her nose on the screen and looks in at me. I guess she is people watching as I am wildlife watching.

Offer Shelter

The third key element for welcoming wildlife into your landscape is to offer shelter. In some cases

Going Native

Some gardeners believe in using only native plants as food sources for wildlife. Where I live, some of these plants are gamble oak, black currants, and mahonias, plus wildflowers like penstemons, wild zinnias, wild roses, and various coneflowers. Studies show that even modest increases in the native plant cover on suburban properties significantly increases the number and species of breeding birds and native insect pollinators.

Though native plants are a wonderful component of any landscape, a strictly native approach will mean a less diverse plant palette when it comes to designing landscapes and gardens. If you choose to go strictly native, do some research to find which plants will be appropriate for your garden design and, of course, which are available from nursery and seed suppliers. A native-plant garden, or a landscape that incorporates some native plants, makes a nice partner for a food garden.

I prefer to work with a diverse list of plants. To provide food to the wild critters around me, I select plants native to my area and other simply great plants that will thrive in the climate and soil where I live.

By taking the time to create a
predictable spot for garden discards,
I encourage the wildlife to look there
for handouts, rather than in the
garden or orchard.

you can provide ready-made houses, but more generally you can allow space in which the animals can build their own homes. Areas of shelter will encourage birds, squirrels, and toads to live in or near gardens rather than just pass through.

All kinds of birds have made their homes on our property. Earlier in this chapter I mentioned the sharp-shinned hawk that lives seasonally in our giant mulberry tree; last year she took a mate and we saw them hunting together in our hedgerow almost every day. Curve-billed thrashers have made high-rise apartments in our giant cholla cactus; they've built three or four nests each season, raising several families in the course of one gardening year. Rosy finches coexist quite nicely as their neighbors in the ferns of the desert garden.

Cottontails have joined the desert-garden community by living at the base of these same plants. I suspect they feel somewhat protected from foxes and coyotes in that thorny habitat. Red-winged blackbirds have made the area around the ponds their neighborhood. They are quite territorial during the spring nesting season. Once the baby birds have left the nests, the adult blackbirds go on a feeding frenzy, devouring beetles, crickets, and grasshoppers all through the landscape. They rid the vegetable and fruit gardens of all these pests in short order. We really enjoy having them on our property.

Quail have also made the desert garden their home base. We see two pairs, with their families, moving through it all the time. The males like to sit on high points and crow like roosters, but with a quail-sounding crow. They are particularly fond of perching on the giant wood mulch pile and on our small garden tractor and telling the world all about their lives! They forage for seeds at the base of the bird feeders. I regularly see them in my vegetable garden, too, scuttling over the lettuces and spinach to catch bugs. They are very speedy

hunters when it comes to catching crickets, earwigs, and flea beetles, and I've never seen them damage any of the plants. I welcome the quail to the gardens and the rest of the farm, too. If the quail and other birds were not on bug patrol, my lettuces might be eaten by grasshoppers and the flea beetles would devour the tops off the radishes and beets.

I have not provided any birdhouses in the gardens. Instead, I have planted lots of shrubs and trees so that the birds feel welcome to make their homes there, as they do in the hedgerows. There are also lots of structures, like our little garden house and the small well house, where they find a welcome environment to build their nests. I have also made available some nesting materials, such as unspun wool and bits of yarn and felt, via baskets that hang in some of the trees and shrubs. The birds help themselves to these materials as they are creating their homes, preparing to start their families.

I don't supply human-made abodes for birds, but I've installed a luxurious bat house on the north end of the seed-storage room. One corner of our farm is a beeyard; a beekeeper friend provides top-bar beehives for her honeybees there. Last winter I started putting out bee boxes for mason and other native bees. (See page 49 for more on nesting boxes for solitary bees.)

You may have other creatures moving through your garden landscape but not residing there. Deer and bobcats have territories that cover a large area. They are constantly moving through that territory; sometimes they pass through more than once in a day. The average person would most likely not even realize that a bobcat passes through each night.

We have a bobcat that ambles through our beds of grapes and perennial-seed crops in summer. We rarely see it. We know it's here because

we hear it at night through our open bedroom window. We occasionally see some scat, too. This creature does no damage to the crops or the gardens. We also have a pair of foxes that visit. I see them each morning moving through the driveway gardens around 5:30 AM. They are welcome in my garden, as the foxes help keep the rabbit population under control. They hunt mice and squirrels as well. The bobcat and the foxes play an important role in hunting other creatures that also hold important roles in the cycle of life. They're part of the bigger picture that creates balance in the food chain so that we don't have problems with any one species getting out of control.

There are likely quite a number of wild creatures living in or near your garden. Many of them may have been there all along without your noticing them. As you become more observant, I believe you will notice the creatures living there and what they are doing that contributes to the health and well-being of your plants. Giving them opportunities to make their homes in and around your garden landscape will benefit all concerned.

Welcome a Toad

I have created toad-welcoming habitat using squatty clay pots, about 12 inches in diameter, planted with shade-tolerant edibles such as parsley and kale in shady, moist areas of the food garden. An empty clay pot turned upside down and propped up on one side also works well. Toads like to hang out where the soil is moist and they're protected from the harshness of the sun. They burrow into the soil just a little, maybe 1 or 2 inches, without disturbing roots or damaging plants. They feast on insects like gnats and flies — and on slugs! Once they've cleaned up an area, they hop on over to a different pot or moist spot of the garden and begin feasting in that location. For such little guys, they really work hard and are great insect devourers.

Years back, when I was the plant propagator for a large nursery in Denver, I worked with a group of amazing women. These women, who came mainly from Chihuahua, Mexico, had all sorts of cultural rituals and traditions for just about everything life might present to them. We worked together in the greenhouses, where there were quite a few toads hopping about. These women believed that whenever you see a toad, whatever thought is in your mind at that instant will come true. They believed that toads are very good omens and that seeing one means that something good or special is about to happen in your life. Every time I see a toad, it brings me wonderful memories of these women. And when I think of all the good and hard work toads do in my garden, helping keep it free of pests, they sure seem like a good omen to me!

Protect Animals Raising Their Young

Often the primary reason a wild creature like a rabbit or a bird builds a secure home is to raise its offspring safely to adulthood. Wild animals lead full but often difficult, short lives. Their own immediate life cycle may consist of just a few days or weeks, several years, or occasionally decades, but in most cases they do not walk, fly, or swim on the earth nearly as long as we humans do. They have no time to waste. For them, raising young is absolutely key to the survival of the species. Like us, though, they strive for their offspring to be healthy and safe, and to grow up to lead good adult lives.

A mother cottontail will try to build her nest in a spot that she feels is protected both from weather and from predators. Baby cottontails spend a lot of time on their own, so leaving them in an area where they are not likely to be eaten by a larger creature is important. The cottontails here nest in places like the woodpile, the equipment shed, or the little garden house. Eventually, though, the babies begin to explore the larger world as they look for food and, once they're grown, mates of their own. Life is not easy for wild rabbits. Their role in the natural world is to be a food supply for coyotes, foxes, and hawks. Their lives are usually pretty short.

Cottontails are abundant in our landscape and would eat a lot of my garden if I were not cleverly planting parsley around the outskirts for their benefit. I enjoy watching the rabbits, and I must admit that I get very attached to the babies, keeping track of their movements to see what they are up to.

The fawns hidden in our hedgerows by their mothers grow up to use our backyard gardens as a giant playground, chasing one another around the fence that protects my lettuces. The mother deer feel safe here, as do the rest of the adult herd passing through twice daily. Sometimes they linger all day in my back garden space, especially during the fall. My homeplace is a clearly safe haven for the deer. I am pleased and comfortable with that.

Many people would be horrified at the idea of 30-plus deer hanging out in their herb, flower, and food gardens, not to mention resting under their fruit trees. Having them around has its challenges, so I do not want to mislead anyone into thinking that deer are absolutely no trouble to my gardens. I take steps to protect specific plants from their browsing, and in this way we coexist in a reasonable manner. The mother deer have a safe place to raise their fawns, and I get the pleasure of their company.

The same is true for the wild birds that nest and raise their young in my garden landscape. The biggest risk to the wild birds here are cats, both ours and the neighbors'. Thankfully, my cats are not big bird hunters, but they have been known to catch wild birds on occasion. When this happens, I put them under house arrest for a day or two, until the hunting urge subsides. I also make sure they have plenty to eat so that they do not turn to hunting out of hunger.

Domestic cats, which comprise both house cats and feral cats, are becoming an ever more serious threat to the survival of songbirds. Large numbers of people own cats, and many more feed wild birds around their homes, which brings the birds into the very spaces where cats travel. It is possible to have cats and still welcome wild birds into your garden, but you must pay attention and take preventive actions. For example, place birdbaths and feeders up on mounds or pedestals and clear away vegetation at the immediate base so that birds can see cats approaching.

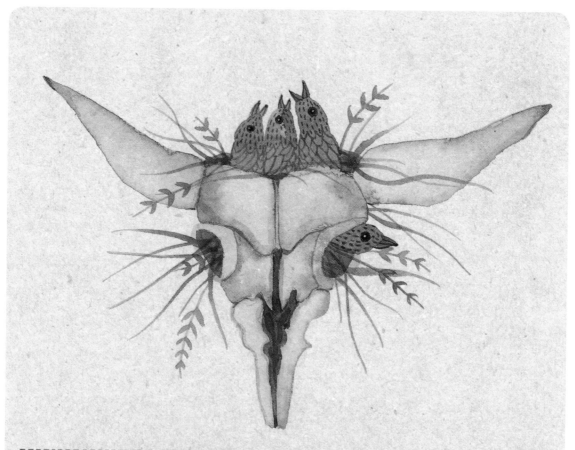

Giving Birds a Helping Hand

We have a quaint old shed of sorts in which we store our hand gardening tools; we fondly call it the little garden house. Nailed up above the door is an old cow skull. Last year I noticed that it was filled with grass, feathers, and cattail fluff that had been woven into a nest. When retrieving a weeding tool one day I heard the sweetest peeping of baby birds. They were raising quite a ruckus asking their parents for a meal. Suddenly, in through the eye socket swooped a parent finch, with meal in beak, and lunch was served. We didn't intentionally create a home for rosy finches, but there they were, raising a family by our garden.

But that is not the end of the story. A few days later I again heard a ruckus in the finch home, but this time it had an element of frantic distress. I looked up to see a squirrel doing its best to raid the bird nest. Well, I was going to have none of that! I rolled some duct tape into a 3-inch tube and stuck it on the only spot that gave the squirrel any possibility of reaching the cow skull. The squirrel did not like the feel of walking on the duct tape and having its feet stick to it, so after about 30 minutes or so of this, it gave up and left the birds alone. The next day I took the tape down, and I haven't seen the squirrel bothering the birds since. I didn't have to do anything harmful to the squirrel, but I was able to annoy it enough to discourage it.

Some people put collars with bells on their cats, but I feel that this practice is dangerous, as cats climb and jump on things where a collar might get caught and they could be seriously injured or killed. I have taken to putting a small fence around one bird garden that my cats frequent. It is not a serious fence, but it is enough of a deterrent that the cats do not bother to pursue the birds feeding within that space. As for the neighborhood cats, we have purchased a contraption called a Scaredy-Cat (see page 106). If a neighborhood cat is hunting, usually at night, it will trigger the motion detector on the device. The cat will immediately get doused by a strong spray of water. It takes only a couple of incidents for the cat to figure out that this is not an area to visit. When baby birds are fledging from their nests, we set up the Scaredy-Cat on the outskirts of the garden.

The other good way to protect young and vulnerable wildlife is by simply being observant. If possible, avoid parts of the garden landscape where you know baby creatures are living. If you can't avoid the area, make your actions nonthreatening and respectful. Be careful where you walk and what you do with that hoe or rototiller so as not to cause injury to little ones in nests. I have found that young animals often hide and stay very quiet as I pass nearby or go about my work, each of us watching the other. Wildlife babies grow up fast, so you won't be inconvenienced long by the little ones, whether they are baby birds learning to fly or young foxes romping around in your yard.

Plant Hedgerows

As I discussed in chapter 3, one of the best ways to encourage wildlife is by planting and maintaining hedgerows. In addition to providing shelter, hedgerows can incorporate plants that are good food sources for many kinds of wildlife. The hedgerow can also contain plants that are edible for humans. Among these are hawthorn trees, chokecherry shrubs or trees, wild plum trees, and rosebushes. Black walnut, piñon pine, and mulberry trees could all fit nicely into a hedgerow planting.

I take extra advantage of hedgerows by using strategic planting of my pest-susceptible vegetables and other food-garden plants nearby. This results in helpful management of pests, because the birds and spiders living in the hedgerow will have a ready food supply.

It is quite acceptable to use the same types of plants I consider good hedgerow plants for general use in the landscape, rather than planting them in a formalized grouping. If you have a lot of fruiting trees and shrubs, they will essentially do the same thing as a hedgerow does in providing food, shelter, and protection for the wildlife that visits your property, without requiring the long amount of space that you would use if you were planting a hedgerow.

On our farm we have planted individual or grouped trees and shrubs in addition to the hedgerow that we have on the north side of our home. On the south side, alongside the driveway, we have planted gardens ostensibly for their beauty, as they are in a public viewing area of the property, but their real purpose is to attract wild birds. This is an arid part of our landscaping, irrigated only two or three times during the year. The plants chosen for this garden — butterfly bushes, mahonia, desert bird-of-paradise (*Caesalpinia gilliesii*), and chilopsis — are xeric (that is, able to live with little water) and long-blooming.

The backbone of this garden is a very old lilac bush that was here when we moved to the farm in 1996. It makes an ideal perch for the birds,

offering them some protection; its numerous branches enable many kinds of birds to use it at the same time. The garden contains a lot of other bird-friendly plants, such as rabbit brush, golden currant, Oregon grape (*Mahonia repens*), Russian hawthorn, and butterfly bush. Bird-attracting perennials in this garden are penstemons, globe mallow, silver sage (*Artemisia ludoviciana*), lavender, and purple coneflower (*Echinacea*). All of these perennials produce seed that birds, especially the little goldfinches, enjoy. Because this garden is specifically intended to attract wild birds, it contains two birdbaths and an array of feeders. The feeders hold Niger thistle, black oil sunflower seeds, and two kinds of millet. We have several of these small bird gardens, in various areas on the property.

Hedgerow Trees and Shrubs

Choose plants that will thrive in your climate and your growing conditions, and that will fit in the space available. (Mulberry trees and most nut trees grow very large!) Here are a few classic choices.

- Chokecherry shrubs or trees
- Currant bushes
- Elderberry shrubs or trees
- Hawthorn trees
- Hazelnut trees
- Juniper shrubs or trees
- Mahonia shrubs
- Manchurian apricot trees
- Mountain ash trees
- Mulberry trees
- Oak trees
- Serviceberry (also called Juneberry, shadbush, or saskatoon) shrubs or trees
- Shrub roses
- Western sand cherry shrubs
- Wild plum trees

> *The last word in ignorance is the man who says of a plant or animal, "What good is it?" If the land mechanism as a whole is good, then every part of it is good, whether we understand it or not.*
> — ALDO LEOPOLD

6 Smart Strategies for Peaceful Coexistence

IS IT POSSIBLE TO REAP AN ABUNDANT HARVEST and still have wildlife in the garden landscape? It's one thing to welcome pollinators and beneficial predators, but what about critters that munch on the vegetables? Can you coexist in a way that provides you with plenty of fruits, vegetables, and flowers and yet does not harm the problematic wild animals and birds that cross your garden path? The answer is definitely yes.

Before deciding whether something in the garden is a problem that must be dealt with, try observing the situation for a little while and ask yourself these questions:

- Are the pests doing real and significant harm to garden plants or just minor disfiguration?

- Do they offer some benefit that justifies tolerating some damage?

- Do the pests have a short life cycle that will limit the extent of the damage?

- Is there a way to coexist rather than driving them out or killing them off?

- Am I afraid of these pests or just uncomfortable around them? If I'm afraid, is it because they're truly dangerous?

- If I must act, what's the least disruptive, least harmful remedy?

Here are some common problems you may encounter, and a few remedies to try. These remedies are being used by gardeners everywhere to redirect problematic insects and animals without harming the natural cycles in the gardens.

Please remember that every garden and situation will be different, so the results from a specific remedy may vary as well. A remedy may work much better than expected, or you may have to try more than one before you find what works best. If you're not able to plant a surplus,

and using a decoy isn't effective, then try a scare tactic of one kind or another. Scare tactics may frighten wildlife, but they do not actually harm them. Repellents, if properly applied, can be a great way to keep wildlife from damaging specific parts of the garden. This chapter discusses simple interventions for distracting wildlife; learn about physical barriers such as row coverings and fences in chapter 7.

Rotate Crops to Reduce Pests

As you plan your garden, figure out a rotation cycle so that the same plants don't grow in the same location each year. This is especially important for plants prone to insects or diseases such as tomatoes, squash, and strawberries. I learned this the hard way with squash bugs. The second year the squash bugs were terrible, and the third year the bugs pretty much ate up all my squash, cucumbers, and pumpkins. Yikes! A gardening friend explained that the insects were laying their eggs in the soil and then wintering-over underneath the straw mulch. I began to remove the mulch after the growing season, exposing the soil to harsh winter temps, which helped kill off the insect eggs. I further helped prevent the problem by getting serious about rotating my vegetables year to year into a different garden bed on a three-year rotation cycle.

As well as helping prevent insect problems, crop rotation reduces diseases and helps maintain fertile soil. It's pretty easy to carry out. In the first year, plant tomatoes. In the second year, plant garlic and salad greens or carrots in that spot. In the third year, plant cucumbers or yellow summer squash. The following year, plant tomatoes there once again. Each year the vegetables are grown in a different spot and not planted in the same soil until three years have passed.

A reason to rotate the garlic crop from one garden bed to another each year is its microbial action: Garlic helps prevent soil-dwelling diseases from getting established. Strawberries should be rotated too, but on a longer cycle. The plants tend to wear themselves out every three to four years, so many growers start a fresh bed at the end of year three. Make the new strawberry bed in a completely different area of the garden, and you'll find you have fewer problems.

Plant a Surplus and Share Some

One of the most effective methods of dealing with pests is simply to plant enough to share with them. For many years I've employed this method because I'm not crazy about having fences everywhere. I like an open feel to my garden landscape, but of course this means that wild critters are able to roam freely at any time of day or night.

One of the best ways I share my garden's bounty is through the hedgerows planted outside the food gardens and the orchard, as well as along the borders of our property. The hedgerows contain many kinds of fruiting trees and shrubs. I selected the varieties so that there is some fruit ripening in the hedgerows whenever there is fruit ripening in the gardens and in our orchard.

For example, I grow Italian prune plums in the orchard and wild plums in the hedgerows. I leave the latter for the wildlife (even though my grandmother made delicious jelly from wild plums). Another example is the Manchurian apricot tree. I have one growing in my garden, which is the tree I harvest from. Others, left for the wildlife, grace the perimeter of our property among black walnuts, cottonwoods, and mulberries.

Sometimes sharing with wildlife means just increasing the amount I plant. In this way, there is usually enough for both of us as long as I check the plants each morning or early evening. I can usually harvest what I need before it has been eaten by a critter.

If there are damaged or overgrown vegetables — zucchini that has gotten too big to eat or greens that have bolted — I will harvest those, too, taking them to a specific location and leaving them there for the deer or raccoons to eat. As I mentioned earlier, at my house this is under the pear tree in the front yard, which has become dedicated to wildlife. Many different creatures — deer, raccoons, squirrels, foxes, quail, and skunks — have come to expect that this is the place to look for vegetable and fruit goodies. For the most part, they have gotten out of the habit of grazing through the rest of the garden. Most animals prefer a predictable situation. They eat plants that are familiar to them, frequently ones with neutral flavors. When they discover that certain plants are especially tasty, they'll return daily to that spot to feast.

Some animals, such as deer, elk, and moose, are grazers. Planting a surplus works best for them; they will browse for a while and then move on. Other animals, such as bears and raccoons, are gorgers. They search out a large supply of fruit and vegetables in one place. Then they stay

*Sometimes sharing with wildlife means just
increasing the amount I plant.*

put, eating as much as they possibly can. When they've eaten all the fruit or vegetables in that spot, they move on, looking for a new place to gorge. Finally, there are those that store food. These wild critters eat what they need in the moment and then haul off as much as they possibly can to store for the off-season. Squirrels are notorious for this approach; they bring back to their home a great deal of booty but also bury it in various places in the area so they have a backup supply. We have a number of black walnut and peach trees that came up as seedlings from squirrel-planted walnuts and peach pits. Having the fruiting trees and shrubs in the hedgerows and around the perimeter of the property is

a good way to deal with the animals that are gorgers and hoarders, as they will find a surplus supply of food at those locations, which are not restricted from their access, and they will not cause as much trouble in the food garden and the orchard.

Distract Them with Decoy Plants

A variation on planting enough to share is planting something to lure animals away from particularly tasty fruits or vegetables. In the introduction to this book, I shared the story of planting parsley as a decoy plant for deer and rabbits so that they wouldn't eat my salad greens. Parsley makes an attractive border around my food garden while standing guard over the vegetables all summer long. Cilantro also works.

Other decoys can help lure insects elsewhere. Radishes are a wonderful example. They'll draw flea beetles away from other cool-season vegetables in the mustard family, plus potatoes and eggplants. Flea beetles apparently find radish tops delicious. If you plant radishes between broccoli, pak choi, or arugula, the flea beetles will almost always eat the radish tops and leave the other vegetables alone. They can eat as many holes as they like in radish tops without causing significant damage to the roots, which of course is the part of the radish that humans want, so this is a winning solution for all concerned.

I'm pretty stingy about sharing raspberries; they're my favorite fruit. I grow a row of sunflowers near my raspberry patch, a cheerful living wall separating the food garden from our flower seed production field. Many birds prefer the sunflower seeds, and that keeps them busy and out of my raspberries. I plant different varieties of sunflowers, with both large- and small-seeded flowerheads. Blackbirds and other large birds eat

Pat's Tomato Hornworm Story

A colleague shared this story about how she deals with tomato hornworms. Tomato hornworms mature into sphinx moths, which are great pollinators for all manner of tubular flowers, such as penstemons and sages. It is therefore in the interest of the gardener to let the tomato hornworms mature.

Pat says she grows her tomatoes in containers on her patio, and she specifically grows one plant just for the tomato hornworms. When the the tomato hornworms begin to show up on her plants, she just gently picks the worms off "her" tomato plants and resettles them on "their" plant. The hornworms feed off the foliage of that specific tomato plant and hers grow undamaged. The caterpillar stage is 20 days, "so it's not that much of a hassle, and we love the sphinx moths," says Pat.

I grow a row of sunflowers near my raspberry patch. Many birds prefer the sunflower seeds, and that keeps them busy and out of my raspberries.

the big-seeded Lyng's Greystripe or Fat Mama sunflowers; for the small birds I plant Autumn Sun or Velvet Queen. Although this won't work for serious berry-eaters like cedar and Bohemian waxwings, it's a great help with omnivorous birds.

We raise flower seed on our farm, and that field is filled with ripening seed that's tempting to the resident bird community. The wall of sunflowers helps keep birds away, but it's not big enough to protect all of the seed crops. I have planted several small bird gardens around our home and the food gardens. These little gardens are filled with perennials and shrubs whose seeds birds love to eat, among them purple coneflower, lavender, and butterfly bush. I placed several bird feeders in each of these three small gardens, and keep them well-stocked with Niger thistle, millet, and sunflower seeds so that the birds have plenty of food sources other than the commercial seed crops.

We intentionally attract wild birds to the gardens and production field because many are expert insect hunters and keep our pest insects under control. They're written into the conservation plan of our organic certification, and we've also certified our farm as a wildlife preserve and pollinator-conservation habitat. In two locations where the seed crops are just too enticing for birds to leave alone, we supplement the decoys with a couple of scare tactics (see page 104). This way we can welcome many kinds of birds and still harvest our seed crops. Bird-watching from just about any location on our property brings us great pleasure.

Add Some Aromatic Plants

Another way to steer away wild animals is to interplant the garden with things they don't like, for one reason or another. Quite often deer, elk, and moose will not forage around strong-smelling herbs such as lavender, sage, and mint. I don't see rodent damage (burrowing or chewing) on squash or pumpkins in areas where I've planted a patch of peppermint. I interplant lavender in my food garden to keep deer away from my carrots and beets. Thyme works well for this purpose, too. Chives are another herb that deer never eat in my garden, so these grow near my strawberries and near flowers the deer really love, like roses. If I plant garlic near tomatoes, the plants are left undisturbed by the deer. Feverfew, garlic, and agastaches (sunset hyssop and hummingbird mint) all seem to have a strong enough flavor that the deer try them once and then move on.

Curry plant (*Helichrysum italicum*) and santolina are two ornamental herbs you can use to steer wildlife away from the garden. Both of these are quite nice as border plants for creating an attractive low hedge around the outer edge of the garden. Browsing wildlife will come to the border, smell the aromatic foliage (they might nibble

A Few Great Decoy Plants

- Radishes lure flea beetles from broccoli, pak choi, or arugula.
- Comfrey lures grasshoppers from basil.
- Sunflowers redirect blue jays, finches, and red-winged blackbirds from raspberries.
- Parsley redirects rabbits from salad lettuces.
- Calendulas lure aphids from broccoli and tomatoes.
- Crab apple trees in hedgerows keep black bears out of orchards.
- Currant bushes distract birds from strawberries.

a little to see if it's tasty), and then move along without bothering other plants in the area.

Growing garlic around plants that are susceptible to insect infestations or damage from rooting and digging critters will often prevent the problem from recurring. If you plant garlic close to roses, you should not be troubled by aphids on those pretty bushes. Lizz, who works with me in my gardens, often plants garlic or onion sets to protect nearby vegetables from browsing deer. It has worked very well for us, and we have a huge herd of deer that passes through the food garden multiple times a day. She takes this approach in her home garden, too, with equal success.

Growing sharp-tasting plants intermixed with the juicy, tasty ones seems to confuse animals. Wild animals tend to leave my chili peppers and sage alone. I plant hot chili peppers among succulent spinach and lettuces. I occasionally find a hot pepper plucked off a plant with one bite out of it and then dropped on the ground, but this doesn't happen very often. This has worked for deer, raccoons, and squirrels. The animals don't come back and try eating them again.

Hose Them Off!

Each summer we're faced with an outbreak of pear slugs on our fruit trees. This tends to happen around midsummer. Pear slugs have a short life, and once they're gone we are not further bothered by them, though in other areas they pop up again in September. They're a good food supply for birds, so typically we leave the task of managing the problem in their care. However, the slugs can drain energy from the fruiting process of a tree, so if they're causing serious defoliation, we step in and take action.

Rather than applying a pesticide, we use a pressure nozzle on the end of the garden hose. A hard spray of water will rinse the slugs off a tree. Once they've been washed off, the slugs die. This is an easy and fast solution. It works nicely with no ill effects on songbirds or pollinators.

You can try the same trick with an aphid infestation. If you're trying to dislodge aphids from vegetable plants rather than fruit trees, you'll need to use less pressure from the hose. You may have to repeat the procedure a couple of times in a week or so to achieve control.

Give Them a Hand

Handpicking squash bugs, beetles, slugs, or caterpillars from vegetables and fruits is quite effective. My adult daughter is squeamish about handling these critters, but we found a solution: she wears a pair of garden gloves.

As you pluck the pests off tomato leaves or snatch them from the base of summer squash plants, you can toss them into a canning jar filled with soapy water. Just mix a squirt of liquid dish soap in a quart jar of water, and it's a deadly bug bath. If it's slugs or caterpillars I'm gathering off the plants, I usually just toss them out into the dirt driveway and within moments birds will swoop down and snap them up, happy to have my help for their lunch. In fact, if the thrashers notice what I'm up to, they'll follow me around the garden to snatch up any caterpillar I toss their way.

Repellents: Smelly Stuff and Hot Stuff

Short of a physical barrier, the best way we've found for discouraging persistent problematic wildlife is some type of repelling agent. We use many that we make ourselves, and we purchase others that we've found to be effective. I classify repellents into two groups: those that taste or smell disagreeable or otherwise irritate, and those that give a false message to the targeted wild animal that a predator or dead animal is nearby.

No matter what type of repellent you choose, keep in mind that most will have to be refreshed regularly, at the very least following any rainstorm. Others can last for up to six months and still maintain their effectiveness despite the rain. Some commercial products that would normally be odiferous to our human noses are deodorized but still maintain their ability to repel wild or domestic animals, whose sense of smell is much more sensitive than ours. Because most birds have no sense of smell, and since they often tolerate eating very spicy plants, repellents typically do not work well for birds.

In especially challenging circumstances, we've learned to combine repellents with other tools to increase our chances of success. Also, sometimes a repellent will work for a long time and then for some reason unknown to me, the animals I'm trying to discourage will just ignore it. Maybe they just get used to it. In any case, be prepared to change what you're using if you find that repellent no longer works the way you need it to. Sometimes a fresh approach will do the job.

Garlic

Garlic is always a good choice. In just about any form, garlic will repel all sorts of wild creatures from garden plants. Almost every creature (besides humans) dislikes the smell and taste. You should be prepared for the entire area to smell like a freshly made batch of garlic bread if you use this repellent. You can make it in any number of ways. Garlic water (page 101) is simple to prepare and works very well, but it does takes an hour or so to concoct. Spreading dehydrated garlic granules on the ground around the plants you want to protect is fast and won't make the area smell as much, but it's more expensive.

Commercial products based on garlic oil can be sprayed on or near plants to repel wildlife. If you don't want to have garlic flavor on your veggies and fruits, spray other plants growing in the same area instead of using garlic oil directly on food plants.

Hot Pepper

Often I am asked what might work to keep squirrels and chipmunks from digging around in the garden beds. Or I'm asked how to keep out pesky neighborhood cats intent on scratching up the soil or, even worse, using it for a litter box. My answer? Try hot chili peppers!

Capsaicin is the chemical compound in peppers (of the genus *Capsicum*) that makes them hot and spicy. A squirrel, chipmunk, or cat digging in soil where hot peppers have been applied will get this compound on their skin and feet. If they don't feel it on their fur, they'll get it on their tongue when they clean themselves. It doesn't take long before they put two and two together and realize that at least this part of the garden is no place to mess with.

Animals dislike the burning sensation a hot pepper causes on the skin or in the nose and eyes. Humans do, too: wear gloves while handling hot peppers, and *don't rub your eyes*.

I prefer to use crushed chili peppers because they're easy to get and not very expensive. Any

cinnamon

hot peppers

garlic

mint

variety of hot chili pepper will work fine, but the hotter it is, the better and faster it will work. Choose something like crushed pequin (bird) or habanero peppers. You can find them in the grocery (ethnic or spice aisles), or you can mail-order in bulk from herb or gourmet cooking businesses. You can purchase capsicum-based garden products; some are designed for use against insects, and stronger formulations are for keeping away animals. If you use a commercial hot-pepper spray, follow the label directions for proper application. You'll need to reapply crushed or powdered peppers if they blow away or are washed off by rain; commercial sprays will eventually wash off as well.

I sprinkle the crushed chili peppers on the ground where the critters are digging. This repellent has kept squirrels from digging good-sized holes in my planter boxes in their efforts to bury nuts for winter storage. I don't mind them burying nuts, but sometimes they disturb fragile plants in the process. This has happened to the salad greens, and those plants had a hard time recovering.

Ground black pepper works almost as well as hot chili peppers, probably for the same reason. As the garden season progresses and the squash, pumpkins, and cucumbers are growing well, that's about the time when squash bugs show up in large numbers. One of our remedies for potato beetles and squash bugs is to sprinkle ground black pepper around at the base of the squash and pumpkin plants. It works well on cucumbers, melons, and gourds, too. Many types of insects, as well as wild animals, don't like being around the smell or taste of black pepper. It seems also to repel raccoons, skunks, squirrels, and rabbits. Doug, who helps us on the farm, buys giant-sized jugs of ground black pepper at the dollar store and uses it to keep squash bugs out of his vegetables.

Cinnamon and Wood Ashes

Powdered cinnamon is a great repellent for any soft-bodied insect pests that are causing trouble for fruits and vegetables. The natural oil in the cinnamon burns the body of an insect it comes in contact with, so pests just avoid it. Long ago my grandmother told me to apply a single thin line of powdered cinnamon along the baseboard and in front of the threshold to prevent sugar ants from getting in the kitchen and into my pantry goods. It works in the garden and the greenhouses, too!

Sprinkle cinnamon around lettuce plants to prevent ants from farming aphids on the leaves, or to keep them from eating strawberries. The key is to have an unbroken line of the powder surrounding the area you want to protect. If there's a break in the line, ants will find the spot and pass through it on their merry way.

Wood ashes can be used in a similar fashion. Sprinkle them on the ground around the base of plants that are being eaten by snails and slugs. I use wood ashes around my strawberry plants when they are fruiting heavily. This remedy works well, though you need to refresh the barrier of ashes after a heavy rain. It's best as a temporary remedy; too much wood ash can raise the soil pH enough to affect how well plants grow.

Mint

Mint (especially peppermint and spearmint) is an excellent repellent for many kinds of rodents. Mice, rats, voles, and moles have no tolerance for the smell and leave the area undisturbed. Mice and other small rodents like to eat root crops, and their digging and tunneling will damage plants. This can be a frequent problem where mulch has been left in the garden after the growing season; they find it a warm home during cold months, with a ready food supply of roots nearby. It also happens in growing structures like cold frames.

If wild hunters are not keeping rodents under control, you can purchase commercial products containing dried mint or peppermint oil from garden centers and mail-order companies.

It's important to replace mint products as soon as they begin to lose their fragrance. At that point they lose a great deal of their effectiveness. Other types of plant-based repellents that seem to keep away browsing or burrowing wildlife are products based on lemon or citronella oil, cinnamon, birch oil, balsam fir, and rosemary.

Scented Soaps and Other Fragrances

Strong-scented soap bars, tied into pieces of netting and hung in trees at nose level, will often keep bears out of fruit trees and discourage deer and elk from browsing on vegetable plants. The soap-bar tactic seems to work pretty well with raccoons, too; it has saved my sweet corn on more than one occasion. Some folks use moth balls, but because these are toxic if ingested, I don't. My mother uses fabric-softener dryer sheets tucked in and around her vegetable garden to keep out wild critters. I've tied these onto our grapevines; they do seem to keep away skunks and deer, but I've watched the raccoons smell the dryer sheets, wiggle their noses, and proceed to eat our grapes anyway. Since most birds have no sense of smell, none of these will help keep them from foraging among fruit trees or berry bushes.

The repellents mentioned so far can be used liberally on food crops without risk, but others are not safe to eat. Make sure any repellent you employ is safe for use on food crops if you're applying directly onto fruits, vegetables, herbs, or edible flowers. Check the label of commercial repellents. Rotten eggs and castor oil are in many products because they're extraordinarily effective. However, if you make your own repellent from either of these, it absolutely cannot be used on any plant that will be eaten, or you run the risk of food poisoning. These products should be applied only to plants that are not grown as food, such as shrubs and ornamental flowers.

Animal-Based Repellents

Repellents made from animal parts or excretions such as dried blood, musk oil, and animal urine keep animals away from specific parts of the garden, but they should not be applied to anything that will be eaten, and must not touch your skin. Hair or fur of predators or humans belong in this category as well. These send the message that a human or predator animal has been in the area, thus deterring plant-eating wildlife from hanging around. Sprinkle it on the ground or tuck little tufts of fur here and there under plants or around the perimeter of the food garden. Apply any repellent that contains ingredients derived from animals to the ground around the food garden, and never to the foliage of the plants. I often apply animal-based repellents on pathways and around grape trellises to prevent animals from damaging my crops. They create an invisible boundary on the outer edges of the garden and protect fruit trees and berry bushes. As a bonus, as they break down in the soil they become a source of nutrition for plants growing in the immediate area.

A brief word about using human hair: If you're looking to use large quantities in or around the garden, avoid hair that has been colored, permed, or treated with other synthetic chemicals. The residues from hair treatments are not always safe for people or creatures of any kind.

Repellents based on musk oil, animal urine, and animal fur create the impression that predators are nearby. Animals that might normally be hunted don't take chances when they smell these odors. Blood- and bonemeal products work by giving the illusion that an animal has died in the area, and many animals will be frightened away by the smell of death. However, wolves and coyotes, even domestic dogs, may be attracted to these types of repellents and will dig where they've been applied, causing much damage. You're better off using plant-based repellents such as garlic and pepper where wild and domestic dogs are frequent visitors.

To protect my orchard trees from browsing animals once fruit begins to ripen, I spread an animal-based repellent on the ground about 2 feet out and circling the tree trunks. If a tree has low-hanging branches laden with ripe fruit, an extra temptation to animals, I put another circle of the repellent on the ground just at the outer edge of where the branches hang. This keeps deer, raccoons, elk, and even bears from finding their way into the trees or reaching up to pull off fruit. I have used these types of repellents also to keep wild squirrels and skunks from going underneath our front porch, and during rutting season to prevent deer from breaking branches and damaging tree bark.

Every day I rake or pick up any fruit that happens to fall off the trees. I dump the drops around the pear tree in the front yard, the give-away food station described earlier. It hardly seems fair to leave fallen fruit on the ground where animals will be attracted to it but not able to get at it because the repellent sends them away. There the fruit would just spoil and attract wasps.

Tips for Trapping

Some garden pests can be trapped. One of the most popular remedies for slugs and snails is to pour beer into a plastic cottage cheese cup or similar shallow container and set it into the soil near plants that are tasty to them. The pests will slime their way into the container, fall into the beer, become intoxicated, and drown. Slug traps may work best in humid climates.

Raw potato pieces are good for trapping wireworms as well as slugs and snails. Cut thick slices of raw potato and place them in the garden where you are having problems. Do this at dusk. Early the next morning, take a bucket and gather up the potato slices. They will be full of

Homemade Garlic-Water Repellent

One of the simplest ways to prepare garlic is to infuse it in hot water. Place 1 large bulb of garlic that has been separated into individual cloves (no need to peel the cloves) in a 1-gallon glass jar and fill the jar to the neck with very hot tap water. Cap the jar and allow the water to cool naturally. Once the water is at room temperature, strain out the garlic cloves. Replace the lid and shake well to distribute the oil before applying to the plants you hope to protect. Don't dilute the garlic water; use it full strength. Adding 1 tablespoon of any vegetable oil will help the garlic water stick to leaves so the treatment will last longer. .

The best way to apply garlic water is with a spray bottle or a backpack garden sprayer. You will need to apply another round in a week or after a rain.

Hot Stuff Saves Drip Irrigation

Squirrels chewing on emitters and tubing for drip irrigation systems is a ticklish challenge. Drip irrigation uses up to two-thirds less water than more traditional methods of watering. For those of us who live where water is often in short supply, this method can mean the difference between success and failure. When squirrels or other wild animals chew off emitters or puncture holes in the water tubing or drip tapes, the whole system will work poorly or not at all.

Squirrels can hear and feel water moving inside the tubing or drip tapes. If they chew off the emitters or bite into the drip tape, they create an instant drinking fountain for themselves. The more holes they make, the less efficient the irrigation. It gets expensive to make constant repairs. It's better to solve the underlying problem of why the squirrels are damaging the system in the first place.

To begin, provide better sources of water in the garden for the squirrels. We place several large clay saucers in the area where they were causing the most damage. We keep these filled, adding fresh water every other day. As extra insurance, we mix some hot-pepper sauce into a bit of petroleum jelly and smear this concoction on the drip line near the emitters the squirrels have targeted in the past. (We keep it clear of the emitter holes, as petroleum jelly will plug these up.) The squirrels have stopped damaging our drip irrigation system, much to Chris's relief! As long as they have their alternative water supply, they leave the emitters alone. As a bonus, a family of black-headed grosbeaks have been enjoying the water saucers, too.

wireworms or snails; you can simply toss the potatoes and pests to your chickens for them to devour. If you don't have chickens, then throw the potatoes and slugs into the trash bin. Slugs and snails are night-feeding creatures and hide in sheltered spots during the day. If you fail to gather them up in the morning, they'll just digest the gourmet meal of potato slices and continue to feast on your plants.

For trapping small- to medium-size insects, place yellow sticky cards or tape around the garden. The cards can be purchased at garden centers and are best stored in the refrigerator until you are ready to use them, to preserve their stickiness. Attach a card to a stake using a clothespin or staple. (A word to the wise: Use a stapler that you do not intend to use again in your office, because the sticky substance will get all over it.) Many kinds of insects are attracted to the sunny yellow color, and when they land on the card or tape, they get stuck and perish. Cards must be refreshed every week or two, as the sticky substance will eventually wear out. These cards are also a great way to monitor the insect populations in your garden, as you can use a hand lens to examine the cards to see what has been caught and how many. Unfortunately, the downside of using sticky traps is that beneficial insects and pollinators get stuck too. We use sticky tape in our greenhouses very effectively, but I've stopped putting it in the garden after I noticed I was catching a few too many butterflies.

Trapping is not a good option for dealing with larger wildlife. It's one thing to catch a mouse in a live trap, quite another to trap a raccoon, skunk, or poisonous snake. In these types of situations, your best bet is to call the local division of wildlife or animal-control authorities for advice.

Serious Slug and Snail Control

Chris and I live on a mesa where soil and weather conditions tend to be dry, so we don't have many snails or slugs in the garden to worry about. Inside the greenhouse, where there is more humidity and soil stays moist longer, we sometimes have a terrible problem with slugs, especially in the cooler months. We use commercial pelletized snail bait in our greenhouses, and that works well. Look for one that contains iron phosphate; avoid those containing metaldehyde, which is toxic to pets and not certified for organic use.

Our friend Ryan lives in a more humid climate, on an island off the coast of Washington state. He has to deal regularly with big slugs threatening to consume an entire 20-foot row of young brassicas. As soon as the slugs find the row, he fries them — two shots each — with spray of equal parts household ammonia and water. As a bonus, the nitrogen in the ammonia feeds the plants.

If you have constant problems with slugs and snails, learn to recognize their egg masses. Finding and then destroying them will make a real difference in reducing populations over time. Do your best to foster wild animals that eat slugs: toads, lizards, birds, foxes, and skunks.

Scare Tactics

For particularly tempting targets, such as berries, planting extras and using decoys or repellents may not be enough to deter pests. The next step I employ is a scare tactic. Often I must put the scaring device near the crop before it begins to mature and leave it in place until the harvest is complete. Otherwise, creatures will not be able to resist eating a particularly delicious fruit or vegetable. Sometimes by scaring animals away, I can change their behavior or travel pattern, and once that pattern is broken there is no longer a need for the device. It is also important once the animals have been deterred from the area or the crop has been fully harvested to remove the device so that the animals do not become accustomed to it.

There are many options for scaring away wildlife. The best solution will be influenced by what type of wildlife you need to shoo off. Scare tactics should be scary enough to send wild creatures running from the target areas. They're usually best as a preventive, especially for animals and crops that have been problematic in the past, so plan to install them before the target crop is ripe.

Show Them Some Flash

One of our favorite tools is bird-scare flash tape, which is especially effective for keeping birds away from berries. The shiny tape comes on a roll and is silver on one side, red on the other. It can be tied above any crop to scare off birds that might otherwise pillage the harvest. Even the slightest breeze will cause the tape to move and flash in the sunlight. Birds find this very distracting and confusing, so they don't land on the crops that are covered over or have the flashing ribbon above them. You should put it in place before the fruits or vegetables are ripe so that the birds never get a taste of the delicious produce or seeds. If

you put it up after birds have tasted the fruit, it still works but not as well.

If you have a long row or bed that needs protection from the birds, pound metal T-posts into the ground at either end of the row and then string the flash tape between them, pulling it fairly taut but not so tight as to break it. You can also tie it to the top of a trellis to protect grapes, tie pieces like streamers to the top of tomato cages, or wrap it around fruit trees in a couple of layers or over the top.

Scare-eye balloons work in a similar fashion, and they're available from many of the same suppliers. These are big yellow or black heavy-duty balloons with large scary eye designs on them; some look like an octopus, with big eyes and tentacles of bird-scare flash tape that stream down from the bottom of its head. Position the balloons on poles above the crop they are protecting so that they dangle around in the wind and look threatening.

You can make your own flashy scare tactics from shiny aluminum pie plates, CDs, or DVDs. Tie string to these and hang them from posts, tree branches, fences, or trellises. Install them so that they move freely in a breeze, as the motion is what makes them effective. We've tried these and they work well, but in truth the bird-scare flash tape is much better.

Yellow caution tape, although not the most attractive stuff, is very good for keeping elk, deer, antelope, and moose from crossing into a garden area that has been surrounded by it. Yellow caution tape seems to work two ways. With its movement in the breeze, it evokes the same confusion in large animals that the moving flash tape does in birds, but in addition, the yellow caution tape makes a loud sound that is disturbing to the larger animals. In strong winds it's downright noisy. It's an inexpensive scare tactic and quick to install, especially good in the short term, as when the grapes are just ripening and fragrant enough to attract wildlife. The caution tape can be strung around temporary fence posts or on either side of a trellis to create a barrier of sorts. We use two rows of caution tape, one about knee-high and the other one at shoulder height. Pull it taut but not supertight. Tie the ends well: if a strong wind comes up, loosely tied ends will simply come undone.

We've been using caution tape for years, not only around food plants but also around some of our seed crops whose flowers the deer are especially fond of eating. We use it quite successfully around rows of grapes when the raccoons become determined to raid them at night. I can surround the grape trellises with yellow caution tape for a week or so and then remove it once we've harvested all the grapes. We read some years back in *Mother Earth News* that this was a good way to protect strawberries from being eaten by deer, so we gave it a try. It works, and we've been sharing this tool with other gardeners ever since.

One Reason to Listen to Rap Music

Another short-term scare tactic that works well for certain wild critters is to load up your portable radio with fresh batteries, set the dial to a talk-radio station or rap music, and set it in the middle of the sweet-corn patch. Or hang it from a low branch of a fruit tree just when the fruit is about ready to pick. Talk radio, which mimics people being in the garden, doesn't scare away birds, but it does chase away squirrels, skunks, and raccoons. Squirrels really don't seem to enjoy sports radio. Deep base notes are apparently particularly distressing to skunks, so if you have skunks in an inopportune location, perhaps under a porch, try playing loud rap music until they leave. While

Seven Favorite Scare Tactics

These tools work both in the garden and in our flower-seed production field.

1. Bird-scare flash tape
2. Scare-eye balloons
3. Yellow caution tape
4. Portable radios
5. Traditional scarecrows
6. Rubber snakes and plastic owls
7. Motion-activated water-spray devices

they're gone, block up the entrance to prevent them from returning. The radio isn't practical for a long-term scare tactic: It might begin to annoy the neighbors after a while, plus it would get expensive to replace dead batteries all the time. But when the sweet corn or peaches are ready to harvest, I enlist a radio to help protect them until I can finish picking them.

Fake Friends

The old-fashioned approach of placing a scarecrow in the garden to keep the birds and other wildlife from coming into the space definitely has merit. I've seen grackles sitting on the pasture fence watching me plant my sunflower and bean seeds. As soon as I walk away, brushing the soil from my jeans, here they come. It's amazing how quickly birds can scratch out newly planted seeds or pluck out tender little seedlings for a tasty meal. It happened for two years before I saw them watching me and realized who was to blame for no sunflowers or green beans. Scarecrows have been a big help — the grackles are not so quick to fly in and eat up the seeds.

If moved about in the garden to different locations on a regular basis, scarecrows do their job. I tend to relocate my scarecrows every week or so. The goal is to give the impression that there are people hanging around. If they think people are present, birds won't come for an evening snack.

Setting a scarecrow in an old lawn chair or placing one in a wheelbarrow that's no longer serviceable will allow you to move them around the garden easily. If you wire one securely to a tall shepherd's-crook garden pole, you can pull the pole out of the ground and reposition it as needed with no great effort.

We've laughed hard as we watched deer cross the road and come onto our property, only to stop abruptly when they caught sight of three willow chairs grouped at the edge of our desert garden. The chairs each held a scarecrow. The deer weren't taking any chances — they skirted the desert garden, giving it a very wide berth. The next week I moved the scarecrow-filled willow chairs right in front of the fruit trees, and the same thing happened when the deer started toward the orchard. For more amusement, many of our neighbors, who walk past the farm on nightly or early-morning strolls, started coming into the gardens regularly to see where the scarecrows were. This went on for an entire autumn, bringing smiles to everyone and keeping the deer out of the parts of the garden where they were not welcome.

An alternative to a traditional scarecrow is imitation wildlife, which can be placed strategically wherever wild animals are intruding or causing damage. These fake creatures come in all manner of shapes and sizes, but typically are representations of predators. There are rubber and inflatable snakes that can be coiled in and around branches of fruit trees to scare off squirrels, birds, or small rodents. The rubber ones often look like bull snakes. I've seen them used in squash and pumpkin patches to keep squirrels and mice from becoming too much of a problem. There are plastic owls that can sit on poles or atop structures to ward off nocturnal wildlife. Hawks that appear to be flying can be secured to tall poles so that they flap around in the breeze, but I don't think these are as convincing as some of the other imitation creatures. All of these fake animals work best if put into place just before fruits and vegetables are ripe. The fake predators should be removed as soon as possible once the harvesting is finished. In this way wildlife doesn't get too accustomed to seeing them and begin to realize that they're not dangerous after all.

Spray Them Away

During warm seasons, we rely on motion-activated water-spray devices to keep neighborhood cats from climbing the poly plastic coverings on our greenhouse. Why cats climb the greenhouses is anyone's guess, but when they do, they puncture hundreds of holes in the plastic, which prevents the greenhouses from staying inflated properly. The spray devices we have are called Scaredy-Cats, but there are a number of similar devices. All of them hook up to a garden hose. If something passes within range of the motion detector, it triggers a sudden hard spray of water. Even creatures that normally do not mind water, like raccoons and skunks, usually avoid them because the hard spray is uncomfortable and the animals are startled when the water release is triggered. Animals aren't hurt by the water spray, just seriously discouraged from coming farther into the area being protected.

The water devices cover a pretty significant area — 25 to 35 feet away. The spray can be adjusted to cover a full circle or just a small area.

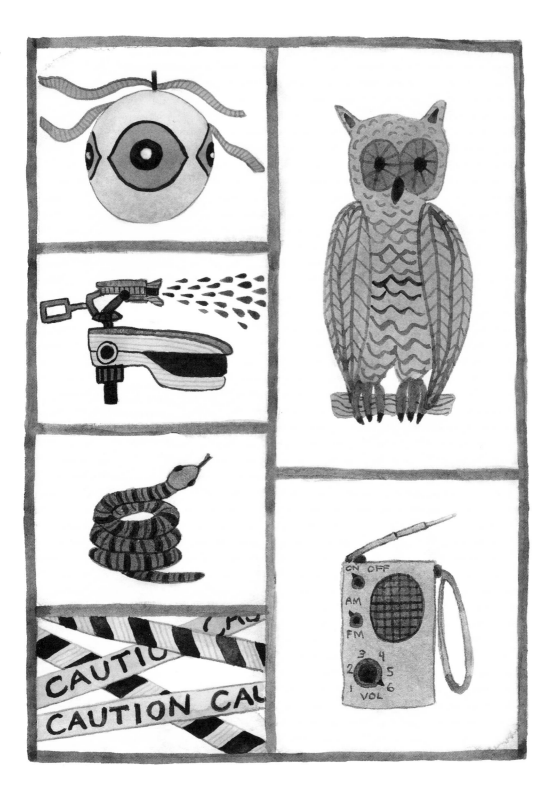

Scarecrow-Building Tutorial

In addition to being useful, scarecrows should also be fun! The first step is to raid your closet for old clothes, shoes, and hats that you no longer need or want. If you can't find enough in your closet, make a trip to the thrift store and be creative about what you choose. Clothes that flap around or move a little bit in the breeze will be most effective. Bright silly hats, dresses, and Hawaiian shirts all make wonderful scarecrow attire, as do Halloween costumes or sports clothing.

Next stuff the clothes into the shape of a body. Traditionally, scarecrows were stuffed with old straw and hay, but you can also use old rags, rolled-up cardboard, or plastic pipes to form arms and legs. Dried autumn leaves work well, too. You get the idea. Heads can be made from stuffed gunnysacks or pillow cases tied at the neck with twine or wire. For heads, I like to use spheres of wound grapevine found with floral decorations in hobby stores. Once I used an old globe and superglued felt facial features to it. The point is to use what you have around that will get the job done and make you smile while you're working on your scarecrow.

After your scarecrow is mostly taking on the shape of a person, get creative about what kind of motions it's enacting. For a traditional scarecrow, nail together two posts to form a cross. Use twine or wire to secure the arms to the horizontal post so that the arms are reaching out sideways. I like my scarecrows to be in positions that people would take, so I sometimes have them sitting in chairs, leaning against structures, or holding objects. Once we created a scarecrow couple that was wired to metal T-posts in such a way that it looked like they were dancing. When you've finished building your scarecrows and placing them in the garden, the next thing to do is watch how wildlife reacts to them. I guarantee it will make you giggle!

These devices can be placed anywhere in the landscape that a garden hose can reach. They're anchored securely into the ground using a spike attached to the bottom. Avoid using them in cold weather, as water in the hose could freeze and cause it to burst. We've had good results using Scaredy-Cats with skunks, foxes, deer, raccoons, squirrels, and of course those pesky neighborhood cats.

The type of scare tactic you choose will depend on the circumstances of your garden and the type of plants that are to be protected. You may prefer a single solution like inexpensive yellow caution tape or you may decide to combine several options within a complicated garden-protection plan for stubborn or difficult situations. We find scare tactics to be valuable tools for redirecting wildlife from areas of our garden during the harvest season, though we might welcome those same animals at other times of the growing season.

They are not lesser than we.
They are simply different.
— MACHAELLE SMALL WRIGHT

7 Blocking Access to Unwelcome Guests

SOMETIMES UNWELCOME WILD CREATURES will attempt to enter your garden. If the simple repellents described in chapter 6 aren't enough to redirect them away from fruits and vegetables, then they need to be locked out. This requires some sort of barrier to entry. Physical barriers range from simply covering rows with fabric or screening to installing a fence or greenhouse. The type of wild creature you're trying to keep out of the garden will determine the choice of barrier.

Temporary Covers

If you have a crop that needs protection from wildlife for only a short time, say, a couple of weeks while the harvest approaches, a temporary covering or screening will serve the purpose perfectly. I've used fabric row covers to protect my green beans for this. We've also covered seed crops with metal screening just for a month or so because deer like to eat the maturing seed heads but aren't normally interested in the foliage and flowers. As soon as we pick the seed, we put the screens in the storage barn. By taking this approach we avoid having to install permanent fences all over our property.

Fabric Row Covers

Row covers are made of fabric, usually white, and draped over a crop or planted bed. Reemay is a common brand made of spun-bonded polyester and polypropylene. Fabric coverings keep out problematic insects such as flea beetles and grasshoppers. They also keep birds and other small creatures from foraging on strawberries or pulling up vegetable seedlings. Our friend Ryan says that scratching birds — towhees, robins, and crested sparrows — used to tear up the hay mulch in his gardens and rip up his pea seedlings. Now he covers entire rows with fabric coverings to protect the young plants. In addition to keeping off birds, row covers will give the baby plants some protection from cold and wind until they get a bit bigger and sturdier. They are quick and easy to install over single crops or entire beds.

When installing row covers, be sure to secure the bottom and ends of the cloth well by weighting down the fabric with boards or stones, or use U-shaped wire staple stakes (sold at garden centers) to pin the cloth to the ground. The downside of row covers is that they prevent pollinators from getting access to vegetable and fruit flowers. For fruiting crops (anything that requires pollination), gardeners will have to remove the covers for some time, or at least fold back one side, to allow pollinators to do their handiwork. Inspect the plants carefully before the row cover is put back into place to be sure no sneaky pests have gotten into the crop.

The lightest row-covering fabric is quite thin, almost gauzy. This type is white and therefore doesn't restrict light from reaching plants. It's usually rated at about 15 percent shading; this small degree of shading is especially beneficial to seedlings and transplants as they're getting established. It is an effective barrier to keep grasshoppers off the spinach, flea beetles out of the broccoli, and cucumber beetles off cucumbers.

Install bird netting so that it's as taut as possible, to limit chances that animals or birds will get entangled in it and be injured or killed.

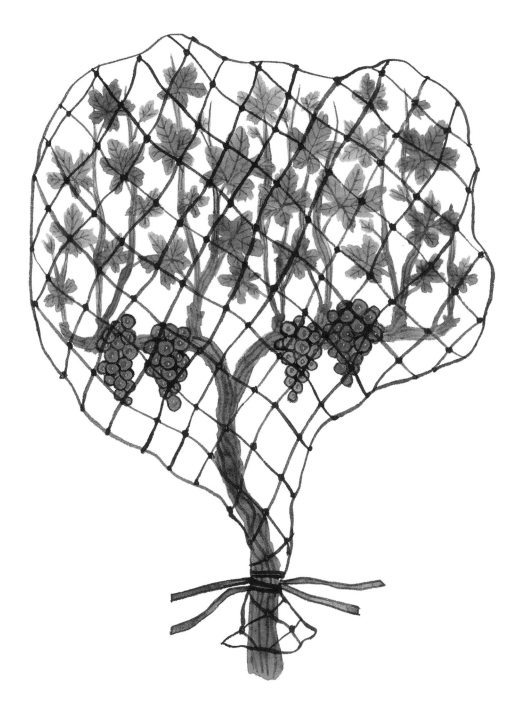

Heavier grades are more densely woven and block out more light (30 to 50 percent light restriction, depending on the thickness of the fabric). In addition to keeping out pests, this heavier cloth offers frost protection (anywhere from two to eight degrees Fahrenheit of warmth underneath the cloth depending on the thickness of the fabric), which is really good in spring when weather is still unsettled or to extend the harvest in fall when night frosts are possible. In dry climates, heavier grades will reduce evaporation but may need to be pulled back during water applications unless a drip irrigation system is in place.

Bird Netting

Bird netting is a lightweight mesh covering that comes in various sizes. You choose the netting according to what size animal you want to keep from having access to your fruit or berries. The holes that form the mesh are big enough to allow pollinators through. As you might expect, bird netting is useful for excluding birds. Usually it's used to protect berry bushes and fruit trees, but it can also be used like a row cover to keep grackles from plucking out newly sprouted beans and sunflowers. Nylon netting doesn't work particularly well for small wild animals; in my experience, they just chew through it. A similar type of netting is sold as deer fencing. Though very sturdy, most netting for deer fencing has 2-inch mesh that allows small birds to pass through it.

Bird netting is often installed over blueberry patches. It's even tossed over fruit trees, especially to protect cherries — which are irresistible to birds. With cherries, timing is everything when it comes to harvesting. If you don't keep your eye on the ripening process and pick the fruit as soon as it's ready, birds will eat it at the speed of lightning! Wildlife-friendly vineyards in California

drape bird netting over grape trellises (secured with zip ties to the bottom wire of the trellis). After harvest it is rolled up tight and tied to the top or bottom wire until the grapes start ripening the next year.

Use care when installing bird netting to limit chances that animals or birds will get entangled in it and be injured or killed. Usually this means installing the netting in a way that makes it as taut as possible. Once I used bird netting over a magnificent sour cherry tree, as I was determined that the birds wouldn't get a single cherry. A sweet little bird got so ensnared that I was not able to free it successfully and it died. Many gardeners value bird netting, but it's not an option I'll ever use again.

Bird netting is handy for containing domestic birds like chickens, turkeys, or guinea fowl within a section of the garden so that they can forage on insects without running away or damaging plants. Chickens and turkeys are wonderful hunters and will quickly rid your garden of crickets and grasshoppers, but they also like to eat seedlings. In addition, as they scratch around in the soil they can damage plants. I grew up with pet rabbits that had free run of the garden. They were delightful, but pet rabbits are no different from wild ones — these vegetarians love to eat plants, especially salad greens. If you have such critters and they're free-roaming, you may need to restrict their access to some parts of the food garden. Bird netting attached to posts makes a great temporary fence to keep them in or out of an area.

Wire Screens for Little Critters

Small critters like squirrels, chipmunks, and rabbits can present a huge challenge for food gardeners because they love to eat cucumber seedlings, strawberries, and some flowers. These critters will either chew through or dig under the edges of row cover and nylon netting, and small rodents will just crawl through many traditional types of fencing. Wire-mesh screening or small-grid wire fencing material is the best choice for these wild animals because it's hard to chew through.

You can easily bend chicken wire or wire fencing into a tunnel to lay over rows or into a dome to protect an individual plant. To harvest, lift the tunnel or dome; simply replace it once you've finished picking.

If critters are digging under the wire screen, dig a furrow 6 to 8 inches deep and set the screen into it. Fill the soil back in and add a row of rocks along the outer edge to discourage further digging. As soon as you are finished burying the screen, sprinkle cayenne pepper or crushed red chili peppers on top of the soft disturbed soil. You will then need to create access for harvesting by cutting the mesh on three sides to make a flap in the top or side that can be folded back. Open the flap and harvest by reaching through the window you've created, and tie the flap closed the rest of the time. Constructing a buried screen with a flap takes some work, but it keeps little troublemakers out of your plants.

Protect Those Tree Trunks!

Young trees are at risk of damage from wildlife until they get old enough to withstand the attention paid to them by deer, clawing animals like porcupines, and beavers and other rodents that gnaw at the bark or try to chew the trunk. One option for protecting a tree is wrapping white plastic material loosely around the lower part of the trunk up to a height of 4 feet.

Plastic trunk protectors installed before winter offer good protection from gnawing by small rodents; just remove them in spring. They are, however, only somewhat helpful with deer, which may be able to scratch the trunks through the wraps. Also, keeping the trunk wraps on long term is not good for the tree.

To protect a tree trunk from deer and beavers, the best method is to build a wire cage around the tree. For deer, leave it in place until the tree gets big enough to withstand the deer. Trunks may need permanent wire caging where

Unintentional Feeding Station

We have a cousin with a beautiful pond in the heart of her perennial gardens. This pond has recirculating water that travels down a small waterfall and along a miniature brook into a decent-sized pool. The pool is home to several koi fish. It is lovely.

A few years back a great blue heron decided this pond was a great fish buffet and made the pond a regular stop for its dinner. The solution was laying chicken wire over the pond and holding down the edges with some wire staple stakes (the kind sold for use with row covers). The stakes make it easy to remove the wire whenever our cousin needs to clean the pond. The wire is clearly visible, but it's not distracting. The bird lands every so often to see if it can fish, but the wire discourages it and it moves on to find its dinner somewhere else. The black plastic netting used to cover fruit bushes can be used instead of chicken wire; it's lightweight, flexible, and nearly invisible from any distance. (Plastic netting will keep out herons, but not raccoons — they can chew right through it.)

beavers are a problem because of stream or creek habitat near the garden landscape.

Fence Them Out

When you want to keep rabbits and larger animals out of the garden, a fence is one of the surest ways to go. The types of animals you're trying to keep out will determine what types of materials and design will work best. Fencing comes in an endless variety of styles and strengths. If your budget allows, go for something that is both practical and attractive.

We're not fond of fences on our property, but we've had to make an exception around the portion of my food gardens where I grow lettuce and other greens. We have mule deer here. A herd of 30-some animals passes through our farmland at least twice a day, and sometimes they stay all day long. In most cases the deer are not too problematic for us, and scare devices or repellents in specific spots are generally enough to keep them from browsing. However, when they see my lettuces and spinach, they think it's the salad bar and simply won't leave them alone. I'm not willing to share my salad greens, so I put up a hog-wire fence around that part of the garden.

Small fences of wire mesh or chicken wire will keep out smaller critters like rabbits. The fences should be 3 feet tall and kept tight. If you're trying to keep out groundhogs, skunks, or badgers, you have to bury the fence underground 12 to 18 inches deep — curving the bottom of the fence to a 90-degree angle, bent away from the garden and running parallel to the ground — in order to keep these diggers from going underneath the fence.

For deer and elk, you need a fence at least 7 feet tall. Otherwise deer will just jump over it. Sturdy nylon netting sold as deer fencing is installed by tying or stapling it to fence posts. In wooded areas, dark nylon deer fencing almost blends in with the landscape.

For the biggest animals, such as bear, elk, and moose, the fence will need to be strong as well as tall. Remember that bears climb trees, so although a fence may discourage them, if they really want in, they'll simply climb the fence. Beekeepers trying to keep bears from raiding their hives often use electric fences. Electric fencing can also be used for deer, elk, and moose. Raccoons will climb wood or wire fences with ease, so an electric fence may be one of the better options to keep them out of a particular area.

Some gardeners have had luck with a tall, solid fence that animals can't see over or through. Deer won't jump into an area if they can't see what's there. This type of fence is expensive and labor-intensive to install. Solid fences work for big gardens, but the shade they create can cause problems for small gardens. Bears and raccoons may still climb over, and groundhogs may just dig under. One gardener friend poured a cement barrier 10 inches deep in the ground around his garden and then installed a 6-foot chain-link fence on top. The cement prevented animals from digging underneath, and the fence kept them from meandering into the garden.

If tall and strong aren't in your budget, consider putting up an electric fence (sometimes called a hot-wire fence). An electric fence is relatively quick and easy to install. First you pound poles into the ground along the boundary around the space you want to protect. Then attach insulator brackets to the poles at regular heights. Finally, string wire at spacing that will not allow an animal to pass through, pulling it taut through the insulators.

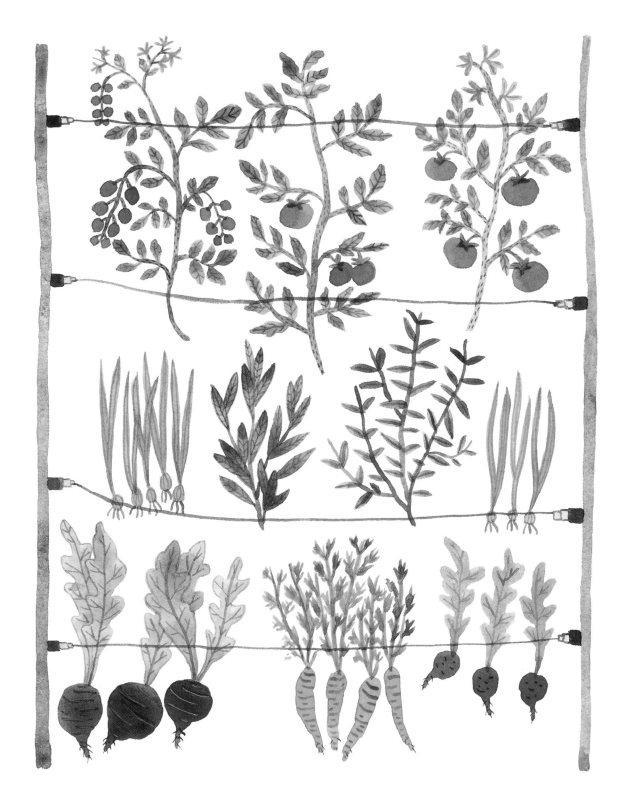

If a tall, strong fence isn't in your budget, consider putting up an electric fence (sometimes called a hot-wire fence).

Once the fence is in place, connect it to an electric charger that's hooked up to a battery or solar panel. Once turned on, the wires will deliver a moderate electric shock to anything that touches them, animals or humans. The shock is uncomfortable and a surprise, but it's not strong enough to be harmful — just discouraging. Deer and moose can walk right through a single-strand electric fence, so for best results it should be baited at nose height right after it is installed. The usual method is to smear peanut butter on aluminum foil strips and attach the strips at 3-foot intervals. The deer will come to the fence to taste the delicious bait treat and will get a shock on the nose or lips. That's all it takes for them to discover that this fence is nothing to mess with. They will skirt it from that time onward. We also tie some strips of white cloth periodically on the top wire so that animals can see the fence before they come in contact with it.

Electric fences work well for all sorts of critters — foxes, coyotes, deer, and moose. In Colorado, the Division of Wildlife recommends an electric fence to keep bears out of orchards and beeyards. To keep out deer and antelope, the wires must be 6 to 8 feet tall. Otherwise these animals will simply jump over the fence without touching it. Because they are pretty easy to disassemble and remove (especially if you use the step-in fiberglass poles that don't require insulators), this is the easiest type for a temporary fence or one that will be moved and reinstalled in a different location as needed.

Cold Frames, Hoop Houses, and Greenhouses

Where weather is a consideration as well as wildlife, as for a mountain garden, it may be worth constructing a structure of some sort to house the garden. Cold frames are great temporary structures for protecting seedlings. Hoop houses and true greenhouses are more-permanent options that involve some cost and time. Any of these will prevent damage to your food crops by large wildlife. Greenhouses will keep out squirrels and rabbits, but keeping these critters out of cold frames and hoop houses may be challenging.

A cold frame is a simple structure, usually box-shaped, that has four sides and some type of lid. It will act as a physical barrier to keep out many kinds of wildlife. They're not foolproof, though, especially the straw-bale type, which may become inhabited by mice. This usually

Vines Enhance Practical Fencing

We use hog wire here on our farm if an area must be fenced off. Hog wire is strong and not too expensive, but I would not call it beautiful. It's a practical fence that goes up relatively quickly by wiring it to metal T-posts that have been pounded into the ground. We use this same type of fencing for grape trellises because it holds a lot of weight if the posts are spaced close together. For grape trellises, we space the posts 4 feet apart, but for normal fencing needs we space the posts 8 to 10 feet apart.

By accident, I was pleased to discover that growing vines of some sort over the hog-wire fence creates quite a lovely screen effect. In this way my practical fence has become attractive, especially when I plant a flowering vine such as morning glory, goji berry, or passionflower.

Hoop houses keep out most wildlife,
especially larger animals.

happens if the cold frames have been left in the same place for a long time. Allowing your house cat into the cold frame on warm days will usually take care of any mouse problem.

You can sow seeds directly in the soil inside a cold frame or transplant young seedlings of whatever types of vegetables you plan to grow during the garden season. Or simply set pre-planted containers or flats in the cold frame. Cold frames work best when temperatures are in the mid-30s or higher. When it's colder than that, plants can freeze inside the cold frame structure.

An essential task to commit to when growing in a cold frame is opening up the lid whenever outside temperatures are in the mid-40s or above. If you forget to vent the cold frame each day, solar heat will cook your plants. I use the same firewood chunk or cinder block that has served as a weight to prop open one corner during the day.

Equally important is closing up the cold frame in late afternoon or early evening, before outside temperatures drop below 50°F. This leaves a bit of extra heat to help insulate the plants against the coldest part of the night. If a really cold night is forecast, toss an old quilt over the lid to provide even more heat retention.

Season-extender hoop houses are like a giant cold frame tall enough that you can walk in. They are much less involved and considerably less expensive than a greenhouse; however, they can't control heat or cold nearly as well as a true greenhouse would. As with cold frames, they have to be vented in the early part of the day before inside temperatures get too hot. They also need to be closed up before temperatures drop. This definitely can put a crimp in your schedule, but a season-extending hoop house allows food gardening for many more months than would otherwise be possible in cold climates.

This benefit may be enough to offset the need to be around in the morning and late afternoon for venting chores. In mountain climates where hail is a frequent possibility during afternoon thunderstorms, a hoop house can provide critical protection for the food garden throughout the growing season.

The simplest type of hoop house consists of metal hoops covered with a layer of 6-millimeter plastic. A better hoop house has two layers of plastic; the air between the layers increases the insulating ability, but this requires electricity to keep the layers separated (inflated) with a small fan. Hoop houses typically have wooden or polycarbonate end walls, with a door in one end and vent windows (which may be opened manually) on both ends for cross-ventilation when solar heat has built up inside and needs to be released. Some people use roll-up sides and end walls. These allow for increased ventilation, but they require more work to open and close.

Hoop houses keep out most wildlife, especially larger animals. Ours have huge square doors at each end that often enable birds to find their way inside. This is not usually a problem. Quail love to hunt insects in our buildings, and red-winged blackbirds fly through as if they're on a bird superhighway. Neither damages the plants, so they're welcome. We had to discourage a robin from building her nest inside, though, because we knew she and her mate would be at risk for being locked in or out at night. We see signs that foxes and coyotes travel through the hoop houses, too, but they seem to just pass through and are probably hunting mice or rabbits.

For gardeners who struggle with large wildlife and short growing seasons, a true greenhouse may be worth the expense. For mountain gardeners, especially, this is a way to grow food year-round. Instead of requiring manual venting, a greenhouse usually incorporates shutters with exhaust fans that run on a thermostat. A heater of some sort helps maintain even temperatures during the night and on really cold days, though heating a greenhouse in very cold weather is quite expensive. True greenhouses have more-traditional doors that restrict entry, so raccoons, moose, badgers, squirrels, and any number of other wild creatures will not be able to come inside and damage the food garden. That said, because the greenhouse provides a controlled environment for growing, it also means it can be more challenging to manage pests.

A greenhouse cat may help with mice and voles, which always seem to find their way in, especially during the cold months when a greenhouse is very inviting and the vegetables and fruits growing inside offer a ready source of food. If you have a greenhouse cat in charge, make sure you put screening over the exhaust fans to keep it from being injured by their deadly blades.

Pests can be managed pretty well in a greenhouse by introducing purchased predatory insects such as lacewing larvae and predatory wasps. In addition, welcoming in such creatures as toads and garter snakes is a great idea because they will eat a lot of insects and even mice. If you have backyard chickens, consider giving them access to the inside of the greenhouse for a few days once all the seedlings have been planted in the garden in late spring. Chickens, turkeys, and guinea fowl are incredible hunters of pest insects. Even mice don't often escape from the chickens!

Building a Cold Frame

You can make a cold frame pretty quickly from scrap wood, cinder blocks, or straw bales. I love straw-bale cold frames because they can be put together in an hour or two and they provide good protection during spring and fall cold snaps.

The lid can be an old single- or double-pane window. Check yard sales or Habitat for Humanity ReStore for old windows cheap. Double-pane windows keep out the cold better, but are heavier to handle and not so easy to find at yard sales. Another approach is to build a lid by making a wooden frame the same size as the base and then stapling two layers of 6-millimeter plastic sheeting to it. Trim off the excess plastic from around the outside of the frame and you're good to go. To keep wind from lifting the lid off the base, weight the lid with a couple of chunks of heavy firewood or a cinder block. Fill the frame with 12 to 15 inches of garden soil or a packaged soil mix.

Each day, awakening, are we asked to paint the sky blue? Need we coax the sun to rise or flowers to bloom? Need we teach birds to sing, or children to laugh, or lovers to kiss? No, though we think the world imperfect, it surrounds us each day with its perfections. We are asked only to appreciate them, and to show appreciation by living in peaceful harmony amidst them.
— ROBERT BRAULT

8 Designing Wildlife-Friendly Food Gardens

DESIGNING A GARDEN IS A REFLECTION not only of who you are but also of what you hope to accomplish. It is an opportunity to be thoughtful about what will work best for the plants so that they may take advantage of your site, to take care of the earth's soil, and to use water wisely, so that the garden grows into beautiful abundance. It is an invitation to other citizens of the natural world — animals, birds, insects, water creatures, and soil organisms — to join you to create something that is more than just vegetables or flowers. It is a painting that is beauty all at once yet also ever changing. The design is just the beginning.

Plan for Flexibility

Designing a garden is a fluid process. The design may shift and change many times on paper. It will change several times again in the process of building and planting the garden space. This is as it should be — since gardens are living places, they can't be held to a strict protocol. The reality is that you will not know everything about the garden when you're designing it. This is part of what makes gardening so wonderful. Every year there will be something new to consider, something to add, and perhaps something to remove. Some things come into play only after you design and plant, because the garden becomes a living community.

As you consider what type of garden design will be the best fit for you, and begin the process of choosing food plants and wildlife-fostering plants, ask yourself a few questions: What kind of garden do I want to grow? This will determine which plants to include. How do I want the garden space to look and feel? Is the garden intended to be strictly practical and orderly or will it be a place also for relaxation or fun? Ponder it. Visualize it in your mind's eye.

Any time of the year is a good time to design a garden space, but I love doing it in winter. It is a glorious way for me to play with the green spaces in my imagination. I bring out my graph paper and colored pencils and sit in front of our woodstove on snowy days, pondering the gardening season to come. What new area will I create this year, once it's warm enough to work the soil? An herb or flower garden? Or a special garden like my miniature fairy garden? My imaginings always incorporate wildlife-friendly plantings and frequently involve ways to expand my food-garden areas.

Designing a garden on paper can be a great deal of fun, because on paper anything is possible! You can be completely outlandish, including things that would look ridiculous or would never work in real life. Go ahead and design your wildest dreams as your first step! Beginning with what seems to be impossible is how a great many successes happen. Plants and wildlife don't read all the books on gardening rules, so they don't care what the experts say a garden should be.

Once you have a plan, sit with it overnight or, better, for a couple of days. After you've had a chance to let it settle its magic on you, go back and work on the design some more. Is it located in the best spot? Will it get enough sun? Can you reach it with the garden hose? Is there anything you don't like? Anything that needs tweaking? Revise your sketch to ensure that your plot is big enough to fit in all the plants you want to grow or, conversely, to eliminate the ones that don't fit into the space available to you.

Once you've put together a design, it's time to finalize the list of plants you want in it. Choose plants and varieties that you know will thrive in your area. Feel free, however, to include a few that are complete experiments.

Think about where you will place items like birdbaths, bat houses, or beehives. If they are too close to where people gather, the wildlife may be scared off and will not settle into the garden the way you hope.

I usually draw in these sorts of things before I start placing plants into the design, but I strongly advise you to be relaxed about it. You may not notice until your plant placement is done that there is a great spot for a bird-viewing screen and a bench behind it, but you can certainly add that into the design as an afterthought. Remember to keep the design flexible and fluid.

It takes forethought to decide where the beeyard will be for the honeybees, so you should draw that into your garden design. However, you can hardly know how a garter snake or squirrel might move through the garden, so nature will just be in charge of that bit. Beneficial wildlife should be encouraged and made welcome within the food-garden space itself. Some wild animals may be fine in hedgerows or orchards, but they may not helpful in other areas of the food garden, and they will need to be restricted from entry to these spaces. Where deer or groundhogs are abundant, for example, it's wise to have a fence in part of your garden design from the beginning.

When I was starting my food garden, I underestimated the need for fencing out deer.

So, the fence came later and was not part of the design process. Now it is in a highly visible part of my garden landscape. It's simply practical and not terribly attractive, although the grapevines starting to grow over it help it look a bit better. It keeps the deer out, and that is my main goal. If I had thought about it when I was designing the garden, I would have built a beautiful fence!

Create a Plant List

As you design your garden, put together a list of plants you are considering. Then draw them into the design where they will be best suited to grow. Think about what amount of spacing they need and how tall they will get. Will they sprawl in the garden, as winter squash and cucumbers do? Or will they stay in a relatively small area, as peppers and cabbage do? Don't forget aesthetics. You may want to include purple coneflower in the garden design for its beautiful flowers; as a bonus, these flowers will attract butterflies. Lavender will draw bumblebees, which in turn will pollinate the squash and tomatoes.

Place trees and perennial fruits, vegetables, and herbs into the design first. Once you have determined where the permanent residents will live, sketch in the best places for the annual vegetables and herbs. Remember to plan for rotating your vegetables to minimize pest and disease problems. If your growing space is small, try succession planting — as one crop finishes, plant another, fast-maturing one in that same location.

A Garden to Delight Honeybees and Native Pollinator Bees

This garden is large enough for several big trees and a plethora of annual vegetables. A wide walking trail curves through the plantings. The design includes a patio spacious enough to gather with friends, as well as a bench at the far end for quiet conversation or rest and reflection.

Many of the vegetable varieties will present a good selection for salads, grilling, or quick-cooking dishes. They include eggplant, sweet peppers, sweet corn, onions, summer squash, tomatoes, cucumbers, and okra. Eggplants are self-pollinating, but they are also visited by bumblebees, which perform a technique called buzz pollination. Tomatoes are also visited by bumblebees, as are cucumbers, peppers, and squash. When these vegetables are buzz-pollinated, they often have larger-sized fruits as a result.

Other types of native bee pollinators will visit many of these same vegetables. Squash bees are great for pollinating not only the squashes, but also other members of this family, such as pumpkins, melons, and cucumbers. Squash bees are ground-nesting bees that will make their homes right at the base of these vegetables. They do not sting, so no worries about having them close at hand. Squash bees do most of their pollinating work just before dawn and just after dusk, when honeybees are not venturing out and are safe inside their hives.

The garden contains many types of herbs, including some lemony ones like lemongrass and lemon verbena. Both are tender perennials, which means you must bring them indoors in cold climates, but they will survive outdoors in regions where gardening can be done year-round. Other herbs such as fennel, basil, and cilantro are nice to have for use in the kitchen. Nettles are grown as a tonic tea herb and to be used as a vegetable in soups and casseroles. Comfrey and nettles are both used for making an activator tea for the compost pile. All of these herbs attract beneficial predator insects and spiders, which will help prevent problems with pest insects.

In the back corner of the garden is a hive for Italian honeybees. Houses for mason and other solitary bees are mounted in the branches of the center trees. Bees are important for pollinating the trees, too. And though corn is primarily wind pollinated, even it benefits from visiting honeybees and bumblebees.

Bumblebees Practice Buzz-Pollination

Sometimes when a bumblebee visits a flower it does what is called buzz pollination. When you are working in the garden, watch to see a bumblebee visiting the flowers of squash, cucumbers, melons and other cucurbit-type vegetables, along with tomatoes, eggplants, and peppers. It will go inside the flower and then it will "buzz" really strongly. This is called buzz pollination and you can hear it when it takes place, if you listen closely. When the bumblebee pollinates using this technique, the pollen vibrates out of the plant and covers the bee. This action causes the flower to get pollinated very efficiently. Scientists have discovered that many vegetables that are buzz-pollinated will exhibit increased fruit size.

*T*his large garden is designed to provide a harvest great enough to fill the pantry with preserved foods, as well as plenty for eating fresh. It includes gathering spaces for relaxing meals with friends. The trickling sounds from the waterfall that feeds the pond are soothing and inspiring in moments of reflection or laughter.

Fences on all sides of the garden would provide privacy and keep troublesome wildlife like deer and elk from gaining entry into the garden. They would also act as deterrents for skunks and rabbits. The appearance of the fences can be softened by the plantings of yams, goji berries, and clumping bamboo, all of which offer perennial edible delights. Goji berry vines and bamboo provide an attractive green screen all year in warmer climates, whereas the yams go dormant during the drier seasons (in colder climates, any kind of annual climbing vegetable or flowering plant could be used). Hyacinth beans are trained to a trellis that borders the patio, providing beautiful purple blooms that attract sphinx moths as well as offering edible pods. (Usually grown as annuals, hyacinth beans are perennial in warmer areas.) Old-fashioned orange daylilies also do double-duty as edible ornamentals. Their leaves can be harvested in early spring before they reach 6 inches tall, and later their buds and flowers are edible, too.

Annual vegetables make up the bulk of the harvest from this garden. Many of them attract pest insects like aphids, bean beetles, whiteflies, and cabbage moths, so it is important to draw a wide diversity of beneficial predators and wild birds to help make sure that pest problems do not get out of control. To this end, the garden has many different herbs, such as chives, garlic, basil, and parsley, all of which are wonderful attractors of those beneficial predators. Lacewings will be there because there are chives.

Beneficial flies, sweat bees, and wasps will visit because there is plenty of parsley, onions, garlic, and carrots. These creatures will pollinate those plants, but also will hunt pest insects.

A supplement to common parsley and chives is the more unusual cutting celery. Easier to grow than ordinary celery, it offers good celery flavor but is harvested by cutting like parsley. Nettles are delicious and nutritious in soups. Both the nettles and the comfrey will provide excellent habitat for beneficial spiders, which also play a role in managing pest problems.

Birdbaths and feeders are placed where they can be seen from the sitting areas. Wild birds will help by hunting the beetles and larger pest insects, like tomato hornworm. The garden also contains a fishpond, which supplies drinking water for wildlife and provides habitat for other water creatures like frogs or salamanders. Water from the pond contains nitrogen from fish wastes; if used to water garden plants, it could supply small amounts of nutrients. Native pollinators will be drawn to the garden by the flowers of herbs, vegetables, and fruit trees, ensuring good yields of fruiting plants. A toad house, too, will make these voracious insect-eaters feel welcome.

Sea Kale

Sea kale (*Crambe maritima*) is an ornamental, edible perennial that can be part of the backbone of your garden. It has huge silvery-white leaves that taste a bit sweet, and it sends up gigantic sprays of white flowers in late summer that look a bit like giant baby's breath. These sprays will be covered with many kinds of native pollinators. Honeybees and bumblebees also enjoy working these flowers. Broccoli, cabbage, and cauliflower, along with other varieties of kale, will also be visited by these same pollinating insects.

Fostering Wildlife with Hedgerows

This garden design has two goals. The first is planting hedgerow habitat to provide visiting wildlife with a food supply as well as a protected place to linger and possibly raise their young. The second, human part of the design is ideal for a garden where only small amounts of vegetables are needed. The unusual circular design is attractive as well as efficient. It provides enough room for a basic group of vegetables, but there are no large garden beds that would require a lot of maintenance.

The focal point of the garden is a fountain flanked by two benches. The fountain is surrounded by a ring of culinary herbs. Next is the outer ring of vegetables. Outside the rings are plantings of trees and shrubs to provide food, shelter, and protection to a great variety of wildlife. The hedgerow offers privacy, and filters out noise and dust from a road. The opposite side of the garden is planted in shrubs and trees scattered more loosely in the landscape, with a table and chair in a beautiful spot to give the gardener a place to relax, read a good book, or watch wildlife.

Crab apple trees and a Russian hawthorn bring height to the garden, as well as fruit for apple butter and haws (the berry of the hawthorn tree) for heart-tonic teas. Both trees can grow into gnarly, fairy-tale shapes. Chokecherry and red currant bushes are interplanted among the crab apples in the hedgerow. These produce berries for delicious jams and fruit syrups to pour over French toast. Lilacs bring early spring color to the garden and incredible fragrance. The wild plums and wild roses also impart glorious fragrances when they bloom, a bit later in the spring and into the early weeks of summer. All of these are wonderful benefits to people, but equally important is that those same berries and fruits can be eaten by birds and other animals. Rabbits use hedgerows as places to build their homes and raise their babies. Foxes and other predators like owls and hawks will visit the hedgerows too, likely to hunt the mice, squirrels, and rabbits living in that habitat.

The lilacs and wild roses will draw in smaller wildlife such as butterflies in abundance, and all manner of native pollinators and honeybees. Although the lilacs will most likely be finished blooming before the hummingbirds arrive, they do offer an ideal space for the birds to build their nests. Beneficial predator insects and spiders are residents of all the trees and shrubs found in this garden landscape. Both beneficial predators and pollinators will be attracted to the herbs in the vegetable garden.

This design makes the garden space accessible to wildlife passing through the property. A source of drinking water is very important, so the design provides a couple of opportunities for critters to quench their thirst. This would be a wonderful design for people who are avid bird watchers, because the diversity of shrubs and trees will welcome a broad community of wild birds. A birdbath and a bird feeder area in and among the shrubs will be a great place for birds to drink and bathe. Because the hedgerow is a source of summer and winter food, a great variety of birds will visit the garden daily and in every season, and nest in the trees and shrubs.

A Dooryard Garden that Welcomes Birds, Bats, and Bees

This garden design focuses on vegetables, fruits, and herbs that grow nicely in an arid climate, but the layout can be used in others as well. The types of wildlife that will come into this garden include many kinds of pollinating bees; honeybees are particularly welcome. Bats also flock to this garden, as do wild birds.

This design mimics the dooryard gardens that are popular throughout the Southwest. The tradition of planting close to the back door for easy accessibility is very old. In earlier times, the entire side yard, backyard, and sometimes front yard could be a big garden. A traditional dooryard garden would contain a lot of medicinal herbs, but this is focused on food gardening. It is more organized than many dooryard gardens, designed to be very practical.

Wood-mulched pathways are wide enough for a wheelbarrow to make its way through the entire garden. The design offers sitting places to encourage people to linger and observe the great variety of birds, pollinators, and beneficial predators as they go about their business. Fences on three sides provide privacy and restrict the entry of large wildlife, such as deer, that would like to browse on the grapes and vegetables. The fourth side is protected by a structure such as a house.

The back fence doubles as a grape trellis. When grapes are almost ripe, the entire trellis is covered with netting to protect the fruit from hungry birds. Because raccoons are also attracted to ripening grapes, the design incorporates a motion-detector water device, like a Scaredy-Cat, to be set up in the mulch pathway and directed toward the grape trellis to scare off the nocturnal foragers.

Sunflowers are planted along the driveway fence and these have been added to the design primarily to attract seed-eating birds to the garden, where they will also forage on large pest insects like bean beetles, squash bugs, or tomato hornworms. Additionally, there are bird feeders and a birdbath to support the avian community.

At the end of the house, mounted up high, is a bat house. As bats fly, they make clicking sounds (echolocation), which can be heard if you are standing quietly in the night and listening closely. Bats are amazing insect hunters, and they are very fond of eating mosquitoes. For this reason they are an important component of this garden design.

Beehives have been added because of the great many fruit and nut trees the garden holds. The almond tree is especially dependent on the pollination of honeybees for a successful nut crop. This design encourages many types of native pollinator bees to forage here. Bumblebees, sweat bees, and leafcutter bees will all be attracted by the cucumbers, lettuce, and pumpkins, as well as the other vegetables planted within it.

The perennial backbone consists of an orange tree, an avocado, nut trees, and grapes — both table and wine. The almond and walnut trees will be very long-lived. Perennial herbs like sage, thyme, and chives are part of the backbone, too, and they will encourage beneficial predators to move around, managing pest-insect populations among the vegetable crops.

A Butterfly Buffet

This garden was designed to meet the needs of someone who has limited space for a vegetable garden in an existing, lawn-dominated landscape. The design could also be used for a gardener who is handicapped and needs raised beds that allow for easy access from a wheelchair or a standing position. The garden allows for large planting containers to be made from livestock watering tanks, placed in such a way that there are wide walkways between each container. In preparation for installing the containers, each tank must be punctured with numerous drainage holes in the bottom. The tanks should then be placed on top of two 4×4 boards that form a solid base. After the tanks are put in place, fill them with a good soil mix.

On one side of the container garden is a berry patch, which could be blackberries or raspberries. On the other side is an herb garden, which will attract butterflies, along with other pollinators and beneficial predator insects and spiders. The herbs are part of the perennial backbone, as is the berry patch. The containers are planted with annual vegetables, which should be grown with a crop rotation that has each container planted with different vegetables on a three-year rotation. This will lessen the risk of big problems with insect pests like squash bugs.

The herb garden includes hollyhocks and hyssop, which will be visited by hummingbirds. Dill, parsley, chervil, and angelica are wonderful for attracting beneficial predator insects — hoverflies and parasitic wasps, for example. Echinacea, hollyhocks, and yarrow are favorites of several types of butterflies. The herb garden will also bring in a number of pollinators, including bumblebees and sweat bees; honeybees may even travel in from other areas. All these beneficial insects will take care of vegetable-crop pests, and the pollinators will ensure that crops are pollinated for abundant harvests.

Berries will be pollinated not only by visiting honeybees, but also by wasps and several native pollinating bees. Sunflowers are a component of the design as a decoy crop to help prevent birds from eating too many of the berries. Birds are welcome in the garden because they will be great bug eaters to help manage pests in the vegetable containers. Once the blooming season is past, several of the herbs in the butterfly garden will produce seed that attracts finches. The lavender and echinacea are also excellent for this purpose.

The hollyhocks and sunflowers provide some height. The hollyhock flowers can be added to salads or floated in a glass of refreshing lemonade, as they are edible. The sunflower seeds could also be eaten, but it is likely that birds will devour all of them. The dill can be added to salads and chopped and sprinkled over a baked potato. Purple coneflower, hyssop, yarrow, lovage, and angelica are all good medicinal herbs.

The garden has some pedestal water dishes that are shallow and designed especially to encourage butterflies and small birds to drink from them. This will be helpful not only to the butterflies, but also to the hummingbirds and the small goldfinches that feast on the lavender seeds. Brightly painted butterfly houses could be put in the herb garden on 4- to 6-foot-tall posts to further encourage butterflies to make their homes there.

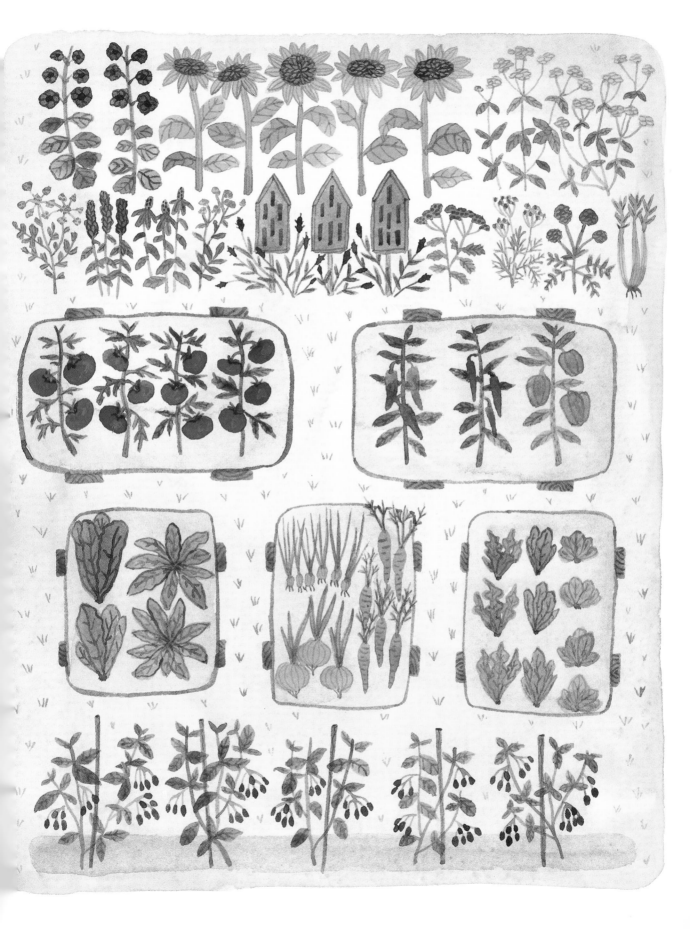

Appendix

Quick Reference Chart for Remedies

Sometimes pest populations will explode despite your preventive measures. If your resident insect and animal predators aren't controlling the pests, you may need to intervene. Here's a list of the remedies described in this book, along with the page number where you'll find the remedy described in detail.

Problem	Remedy
Ants	• cinnamon, 99
Aphids	• calendula decoy, 94 • hose off with jet of water, 96 • planting garlic, 96
Bears	• crabapple decoy, 94 • fencing, 115, 117 • repellents: soap bars, eggs, castor oil, hair, 100–101
Beavers	• wire cages around tree trunks, 114
Beetles, flea	• herbs that repel, 43 • radish decay, 92, 94 • row covers, 111
Beetles, potato	• row covers, 111
Birds eating fish	• netting or wire mesh over pond, 114
Birds eating seedlings, fruit, vegetables, or seeds	• bird netting, 113 • bird-scare flash tape, scare-eye balloons, 104 • CDs, pie tins, 104 • plastic/rubber predators, 106 • radio, scarecrow, 105 • row covers, 111 • sunflowers and currants decoys, 92, 94
Caterpillars	• handpicking, 96
Cats	• birdbath tactic, 82 • repellent: chili peppers, 97 • Scaredy-Cat device, 106
Chipmunks	• hoop house, greenhouse, 117 • repellents: garlic, chili peppers, 97 • repellents: soap bars, eggs, castor oil, hair, 100 • wire/mesh screening, 113

Problem	Remedy
Coyotes	• Scaredy-Cat device, 106
Deer, Elk, Moose, Antelope	• fencing, 113, 115, 117 • hoop house, greenhouse, 117 • radio, 105 • repellents: soap bars, eggs, castor oil, chili peppers, garlic, 97, 100 • repellents with animal and human ingredients, hair, 100 • row covers, 111 • scarecrow, 106 • Scaredy-Cat device, 106 • soap bars, 100 • wraps, wire cages around tree trunks, 114 • yellow caution tape, 104
Foxes	• Scaredy-Cat device, 106
Grasshoppers	• comfrey decoy, 94 • horseradish decoy, 61 • row covers, 111
Groundhogs	• fencing, 115
Insect eggs in soil	• crop rotation, 89 • mulch, 34
Mice, Voles, Moles, Rats	• repellents: aromatic herbal essential oils, dried mint, 61, 99 • wire/mesh screening, 113
Mosquitoes	• *Bt* (specific formulations only), 64 • repellent: mint, 43
Pear slugs	• hose off with jet of water, 96
Pill bugs eating strawberries	• straw mulch, 41
Porcupines	• tree protectors/wraps, 114
Rabbits	• fencing, 115 • greenhouse, 117 • parsley decoy, 92, 94 • repellents: eggs, castor oil, hair, black pepper, 99–100 • row covers, 111 • wire/mesh screening, 113
Raccoons	• bird-feeder strategy, 76 • flash tape, 105 • hoop house, greenhouse, 117, 120 • radio, 105 • repellents: soap bars, eggs, castor oil, 100 • repellents: chili pepper, black pepper, 96, 99 • repellents with animal and human ingredients, 100 • Scaredy-Cat device, 106 • wire mesh over pond, 114

Problem	Remedy
Skunks	• fabric dryer sheets, 100
	• fencing, 115
	• hoop house, greenhouse, 117
	• radio, 105
	• repellents: garlic, black pepper, eggs, castor oil, 97, 99, 100
	• repellents with animal and human ingredients, hair, 100–101
	• Scaredy-Cat device, 109
	• netting or wire mesh over pond, 114
Slugs, Snails	• ammonia, pelletized snail bait, 103
	• beer traps, 101
	• handpicking, 96
	• potato trap, 101
	• wood ashes, 99
Squash bugs	• crop rotation, 89
	• handpicking, 96
	• repellent: black pepper, 99
	• repellent: garlic, 43
Squirrels	• duct tape, 84
	• greenhouse, 117
	• imitation wildlife, 106
	• radio, 105
	• repellents: chili peppers, black pepper, 99
	• repellents: animal based, 101
	• wire/mesh screening, 113
	• water-and-chili-pepper remedy for drip irrigation, 102
Wasps, Hornets	• duct taping clothesline poles, 61
Wireworms	• potato trap, 101

Resources

Garden Supplies

A. M. Leonard's Gardeners Edge
888-556-5676
www.gardenersedge.com
Tools, wildlife gardening aids

Arbico Organics
800-827-2847
www.arbico-organics.com
Tools, wildlife gardening aids, organic garden supplies, pond supplies

Beneficial Insectary
800-477-3715
www.insectary.com
Beneficial insects

Gardener's Supply Company
888-833-1412
www.gardeners.com
Tools, wildlife gardening aids, organic gardening supplies

Gardens Alive!
513-354-1482
www.gardensalive.com
Environmentally responsible products

Growers Supply
Engineering Services & Products Company
800-245-9881
www.growerssupply.com
Tools, wildlife gardening aids, organic gardening supplies, garden structures, and materials

Johnny's Selected Seeds
877-564-6697
www.johnnyseeds.com
Tools, wildlife gardening aids, organic gardening supplies, seeds

M&R Durango
800-526-4075
www.goodbug.com
Organic insecticide for natural grasshopper control

Peaceful Valley Farm Supply
888-784-1722
www.groworganic.com
Tools, wildlife gardening aids, organic gardening supplies, seeds and fruit trees, beneficial insects

Planet Natural
800-289-6656
www.planetnatural.com
Wildlife gardening aids, organic gardening supplies, beneficial insects

Real Goods
800-919-2400
http://shop.realgoods.com
Wildlife gardening aids, organic gardening supplies and structures

Seed Companies

Ark Institute
800-255-1912
www.arkinstitute.com
Non-GMO, non-hybrid seeds

Baker Creek Heirloom Seed Co.
417-924-8917
www.rareseeds.com
Heritage vegetable and flower seeds

Bountiful Gardens
707-459-6410
www.bountifulgardens.org
Heirloom, untreated, open-pollinated seeds for
sustainable growing

Fedco Seeds
207-426-9900
www.fedcoseeds.com
Untreated vegetable, herb, and flower seeds

Horizon Herbs
541-846-6704
www.horizonherbs.com
Herb seeds

Irish Eyes Garden Seeds
509-933-7150
http://irisheyesgardenseeds.com
Organic seeds, potato and garlic starts

Johnny's Selected Seeds
877-564-6697
www.johnnyseeds.com
Seeds, potato and garlic starts, gardening supplies

J. W. Jung Seed Company
800-297-3123
www.jungseed.com
Seeds, bulbs, vegetables, shrubs

Native Seeds/SEARCH
520-622-5561
www.nativeseeds.org
Native seeds of the southwestern United States
and northern Mexico

Seed Savers Exchange
563-382-5990
www.seedsavers.org
Heritage seeds, potato and garlic starts

Insect Identification

BugGuide
Department of Entomology, Iowa State
University
http://bugguide.net
Online help for identifying insects and other bugs

Vegetable IPM
Department of Entomology, Texas A&M
University
http://vegipm.tamu.edu
Online information on integrated pest
management

Educational and Networking Resources

Butterfly Pavilion
303-469-5441
www.butterflies.org
Denver-area science center focusing on butterflies
and other invertebrates

Cary Institute of Ecosystem Studies
845-677-5343
www.caryinstitute.org
Northeastern environmental research
organization

National Wildlife Federation
800-822-9919
www.nwf.org
National nonprofit devoted to protecting wildlife

United Plant Savers
802-476-6467
www.unitedplantsavers.org
Organization for protection of native medicinal
plants

Recommended Reading

Bartley, Jennifer R. *Designing the New Kitchen Garden: An American Potager Handbook.* Timber Press, 2006.

Borror, Donald J., and Richard E. White. *A Field Guide to Insects: America North of Mexico.* Houghton Mifflin, 1970.

Buchmann, Stephen L., and Gary Paul Nabhan. *The Forgotten Pollinators.* Island Press, 1996.

Burris, Judy, and Wayne Richards. *The Life Cycles of Butterflies.* Storey Publishing, 2006.

Cranshaw, Whitney. *Garden Insects of North America.* Princeton University Press, 2004.

Flint, Mary Louise, and Steve H. Dreistadt. *Natural Enemies Handbook: The Illustrated Guide to Biological Pest Control.* University of California Press, 1998.

Fox, Roland. *The Gardener's Book of Pests and Diseases.* Batsford, 1997.

Garland, Sarah. *The Herb Garden.* Penguin Books, 1984.

Gettle, Jere, and Emilee Gettle. *The Heirloom Life Gardener.* Hyperion, 2011.

Hartung, Tammi. *Homegrown Herbs.* Storey Publishing, 2011.

Helyer, Neil, Kevin Brown, and Nigel D. Cattlin. *A Color Handbook of Biological Control in Plant Protection.* Timber Press, 2003.

Lowenfels, Jeff, and Wayne Lewis. *Teaming with Microbes,* rev. ed. Timber Press, 2010.

Marshal Bradley, Fern, Barbara W. Ellis, and Deborah L. Martin, eds. *The Organic Gardener's Handbook of Natural Insect and Disease Control,* rev. ed. Rodale Press, 2009.

Martin, Laurelynn G., and Byron E. Martin. *Growing Tasty Tropical Plants.* Storey Publishing, 2010.

Milne, Lorus Johnson, and Margery Joan Greene Milne. *National Audubon Society Field Guide to North American Insects and Spiders.* A. A. Knopf, 1980.

Mollison, Bill. *Permaculture: A Designers' Manual.* Tagari Publications, 1988.

Nottridge, Rhoda. *Wildlife Gardening.* The Crowood Press, 2009.

Overy, Angela. *Sex in Your Garden.* Fulcrum Publishing, 1997.

Putnam, Patti, and Milt Putnam. *North America's Favorite Butterflies.* Willow Creek Press, 1997.

Toensmeier, Eric. *Perennial Vegetables.* Chelsea Green Publishing, 2007.

The Xerces Society. *Attracting Native Pollinators.* Storey Publishing, 2011.

Index

Page numbers in *italics* indicate photos.

Other Storey Titles
You Will Enjoy

Also by Tammi Hartung

Homegrown Herbs
A complete guide to growing and using more than 100 herbs for beauty, flavor, and health.
256 pages. Paper. ISBN 978-1-60342-703-6.

....

Backyard Foraging by Ellen Zachos
Photographic profiles and harvesting information — including advice on safety and sustainability — for 65 surprisingly edible plants.
240 pages. Paper. ISBN 978-1-61212-009-6.

The Gardener's A–Z Guide to Growing Organic Food
by Tanya L. K. Denckla
An invaluable resource for growing, harvesting, and storing 765 varieties of vegetables, fruits, herbs, and nuts.
496 pages. Paper. ISBN 978-1-58017-370-4.

Keeping a Nature Journal by Clare Walker Leslie & Charles E. Roth
Simple methods for capturing the living beauty of each season.
224 pages. Paper with flaps. ISBN 978-1-58017-493-0.

The Secret Lives of Backyard Bugs by Judy Burris and Wayne Richards
A one-of-a-kind look at amazing butterflies, moths, spiders, dragonflies, and other insects.
136 pages. Paper. ISBN 978-1-60342-563-6.

The Year-Round Vegetable Gardener by Niki Jabbour
How to grow your own food 365 days a year, no matter where you live!
256 pages. Paper. ISBN 978-1-60342-568-1.
Hardcover. ISBN 978-1-60342-992-4.

These and other books from Storey Publishing are available
wherever quality books are sold or by calling 1-800-441-5700.
Visit us at www.storey.com or sign up for our newsletter
at *www.storey.com/signup*.